Gloria Stargel tells heart-warming stories about cats, worn yellow socks, a silver belt buckle, kudzu, and lemon pie. She writes of miracles in her life, in her family, and in the lives of a few celebrities. Most of the stories revolve among the everyday, not-famous people—individuals open for God to work miracles in their lives.

Cecil Murphey
Author and co-author of more than 100 books, including the *New York Times* best-seller, *90 Minutes in Heaven* and *Gifted Hands: The Ben Carson Story*

Gloria does it again—brings us closer to our faith though stories of faith. Beginning with the dedication to her grandson serving in the Marine Corps to the final page, Gloria's stories of faith warm the heart. *My Anchor Holds* is the anchor we need in these troubling times with a message of hope for the future. And that hope is the grace of Jesus Christ.

Martha Zoller
The Martha Zoller Show
Georgia News Network

Everyone loves a good story. A good story can inspire, challenge, or motivate. *My Anchor Holds* paints beautiful and powerful stories that will cause a reader to pause and reflect on the most important things of life....

Dr. Tom Smiley, Senior Pastor
Lakewood Baptist Church
Author, *Overcoming Life's Undercurrents*
Founding President, "Life With Smiles Ministry"

No one is a greater master of the heartfelt inspirational story than award-winning author Gloria Stargel. *My Anchor Holds —The Difference Jesus Makes* contains the best of her best— captivating yet oh so practical tales that are richly reminiscent of the life-changing parables our Savior told. Through her stories of persons sailing the often stormy seas of life, readers will experience Jesus anew. He will become their Captain, their Lighthouse, their Anchor and Hope, Lifeline and Power. And they will never be the same. I know. I am one of them.

Roberta Messner, R.N., Ph.D.
Inspirational and Medical Writer
Regular Contributor to *Guideposts* and *Daily Guideposts*

This book captures the very heartbeat of Christianity: Jesus Christ at work in everyday lives. Addressing universal needs, each gripping true story illustrates how Jesus makes a difference to anyone, anywhere."

LeAnn Thieman
Coauthor *Chicken Soup for the Christian Woman's Soul*

My Anchor Holds is a wonderful collection of true stories that are about how faith and trust in Jesus turn peoples' lives around. They cross all sections of society, and I found them very inspirational. I highly recommend this collection to all who are seeking faith, trust, and hope.

Tommy Aaron
Winner 1973 Masters Golf Tournament

My *A*nchor Holds
The Difference Jesus Makes

Gloria Cassity Stargel

Bridge-Logos
Alachua, Florida 32615

Bridge-Logos

Alachua, FL 32615USA

My Anchor Holds
by Gloria Cassity Stargel

Library of Congress Catalog Card Number: 2008938161
International Standard Book Number 978-0-88270-612-2

Except for Bible verses and short quotes (as credited), all material in this volume was written by Gloria Cassity Stargel.

Cover concept by Jeannine Rice.

G218.316.N.m812.35240

Dedication

To
Our Grandson
PFC Richard Cassity Stargel, Jr.
United States Marine Corps
and
In Loving Memory of
My Mother
Mae Bell Thompson Cassity

Acknowledgements

M y sincere appreciation goes to all those who helped bring this book to life.

First, to each of you who granted me the honor of writing your story: You allowed me into your head and your heart, a trust I consider sacred. Living your captivating accounts transported me to distant realms, unique experiences. Thank you.

Deep gratitude goes to my husband who watched me disappear into my home office—day after day, night after night—leaving him to wash dishes, unload the clothes dryer, and watch television alone. Joe, I hope you will consider those sacrifices to be unto the Lord, and know that for any good resulting from my work, you are an integral part. It may be *my* writing, but it's *our* ministry.

To our children Lisa, Rick, and Randy: thank you for always being there for me, especially for answering my many computer questions.

Special thanks to Norman Rohrer who critiqued the manuscript with much grace, then delivered an inspired Foreword. A sincere thank you to Clara Martin for her continued interest in my work; Roberta Messner for her professional input when requested; Charlotte Hancock who proofed the stories with a sweet spirit; Carol White who made certain the quoted material was accurately referenced; Sisters in Sonlight, my Bible Study group, for their prayers and research assistance; Becky and Ernest Dadisman, Rita Salas, Jane Lawson and other friends, who contributed wonderful ideas for titles; Northeast Georgia Writers for sustaining encouragement; and to Gloria Colter, Azalee Kapiloff and Kelly Baker for serving as my sounding boards during the long process.

To that one I'll probably remember only *after* the book has gone to press, please accept my humble apology and heartfelt gratitude. And to every person through the years who asked me, "Are you still writing?"—thank you for spurring me on.

Above all, I thank God, His Son, and His Holy Spirit who directed the work. The miracles in my life, wrought by this Three-in-One Trinity, are what prompted, inspired, and made possible this collection of my writings.

To God be the Glory!

Contents

CHAPTER 1

Jesus, Our Captain
Learning to Give Him the Helm

CHAPTER 2

Jesus, Our Lighthouse
Heeding His Guidance

CHAPTER 6

Jesus, Our Refuge
Resting in His Safe Harbor

CHAPTER 7

Jesus, Our Power
He is the Wind Beneath Our Wings

Afterglow

Foreword

A skillful musician places her fingers upon the keyboard and from the organ come the whispering of the wind, the crash and thunder of the storm, the tramp of armies, the chiming of the bell and even sobbing as from a heart torn with grief—all arising from a musical score.

In *The Difference Jesus Makes,* Gloria Stargel captures in print the drama of people who have experienced the depth of despair and the heights of joy: concert violinist, plumber, military pilot, truck driver, registered nurse, gospel singer.... Their experiences take place in Yugoslavia and Vietnam, Texas and New York, Atlanta and Alaska—even the South Pole.

How does the Prisoner of War in isolation for five years retain his sanity? What set a juvenile delinquent on the path to recovery from drugs or a mother to find her two-year-old daughter lost overnight in a mountainous forest?

In these slivers of true adventure lies the drama of the abundant life that Jesus promises. Ordinary people experience these encounters while taking a walk, while portraying an angel in the Nativity Scene at Christmas, while weaving kudzu baskets....

Gloria Stargel, a victim of cancer who experienced healing under the good hand of the lord, reveals Him not "in the watch fires of a hundred circling camps" but as divine surprises in the tedium of the routine and the smallest acts that give His Truth luster and make divine wisdom smile.

—Norman B. Rohrer
Author, Founder, Christian Writers Guild

The Story Behind the Book

Who, me? Walk on water!

*"Whenever Jesus calls someone to get out of the boat,
He gives the power to walk on the water."*
—John Ortberg, "If You Want to Walk on Water"

"What's the matter?" my husband Joe asked as we sat at the dinner table.

"I'm wondering what to do next," I said, feeling drained of energy. A year earlier, Joe had been diagnosed with a rare, virtually incurable, cancer, and we had spent the months fighting for his life.

Finally, aggressive chemotherapy and radiation, backed by much pleading prayer, managed to put the disease into remission, whereupon the oncologist had adopted a wait-and-see attitude. The sudden quietness in our lives was like living in the eye of a number five hurricane.

"Now that we have a lull, I don't know what to do," I told Joe. "When you became ill, I gave up my job to care for you ... the boys will leave soon for college ... suddenly, I lack direction."

"Why don't *you* go back to school, too?" Joe offered.

"Do *what!?*" I responded, taken aback. "You know, of course, it's been a mighty long time since I was a student."

I'll admit, though, that the idea of a fresh environment, of escaping the constant cancer concern at our house, held a certain appeal. Besides, I knew Joe worried that I was ill prepared to earn a living if cancer should win the fight.

Change of direction does not come easy for me. Having faced Joe's life-threatening illness, however, I saw the futility of *my* plans. I had begun learning to trust God and *His* plans for me. I earnestly wanted to trust Him in all areas of life. But first I needed to know who *I* was—to find *me*. The words of Saint Augustine express the yearnings of my heart, "Let me know thee, Lord, and let me know myself."

In this new stance of learning to trust, now that the subject of college had come up, I asked God for guidance. His answer was not a gentle nudge, but a strong shove. All the right doors began to open; even a scholarship appeared. The day an astonished me, a first-quarter sophomore, returned to college, I felt a kinship to the disciple Peter when he dared to climb out of the boat and walk on water toward Jesus.

I approached the first classes with fear and trembling. Could I still think? Could I still learn? "Please Lord, don't leave me now, or I'll sink for sure."

As days became weeks, and weeks quarters, the totally unexpected happened. College became, for me, a spiritual experience—one that changed me and my life completely. One that gave me the inner security I craved. The key, I think, was obedience.

The turning point came during my junior year when I felt God was directing me to study journalism. For several months I doggedly continued my social work studies. Surely I had imagined God's message. "After all," I argued, "I'm not a youngster anymore. What would *I* do with *journalism?*"

I'm grateful He didn't give up on me. I felt no peace until I went to my knees in surrender and changed my major field of study from social work to journalism.

Years earlier I had accepted Jesus as my Savior; now I accepted Him as my Lord. I thought I was really sacrificing. But to my surprise, it was my gain. For upon my surrender, the Holy Spirit took control. The more I gave up my will to God's will, the more I felt the presence of the Holy Spirit. What joy to know He dwells within.

One of the first things the Spirit taught me was a life-changing truth: God *loves* me. Now if God loves me, that makes me somebody rather special. I don't need to question anymore who I am. I'm a child of the *King*! What a freeing revelation—freeing from the chains of my own self-doubts. I gave Him the old insecure me; He gave me a freedom I had never known.

In his book, *Let God Love You,* Lloyd J. Ogilvie writes. "Obedience to our Lord is the continuous new beginning of unpredictable possibilities."

One such unpredictable possibility became reality for me when, after three years on campus, I received a degree in Social Work/Journalism. That was one exciting day! And Joe was there to share it!

In spite of the fact that Joe's health had not yet been declared "all clear," life for me became a thrilling adventure with God in control. When I asked expectantly, "What are we doing tomorrow, Lord?," He sent me on a mission to share His love through the written word, telling personal experience stories— my own and others'—of faith at work in lives today.

I have gathered many of those stories in this volume. They have greatly enriched my own life—I pray they do the same for you.

Introduction

*D*oes Jesus make a difference? "Yes," these gripping stories confirm it. As we sail the sea of life we seek security of spirit, an anchor in the storm, Jesus provides these, and more, when we let Him be our Captain, our Lighthouse, our Lifeline, our Anchor, our Hope, our Refuge—our Power.

As you read our true stories, you will laugh—and you will cry, for many are wrought from traumatic, life-altering experiences.

The stories and their locations are as diverse as the individuals who share them. Yet, they all have one thing in common—Jesus makes the difference.

Here you will find soul-lifting assurance that the Lord Jesus Christ calms the turbulence when seas get rough, all the while giving everyday life purpose, direction, and fulfillment. This is the essence of *My Anchor Holds: The Difference Jesus Makes.*

May He grant you hope, peace and joy for your own journey—your journey on the sea of life.

EDITORIAL NOTE: With the exception of those quotes duly noted, all material in this book was written by Gloria Cassity Stargel. The "as-told-to" stories are based on interviews and research conducted by the author.

CHAPTER 1

Jesus, Our Captain

Learning to Give Him the Helm

O Love that wilt not let me go
I rest my weary soul in thee;
I give Thee back the life I owe,
That in thine ocean depths its flow
May richer, fuller be.

George Matheson, 1842–1906
Albert L. Peace, 1844–1912

"O Love That Wilt Not Let Me Go"
Baptist Hymnal, © 1956 Convention Press, Nashville, TN

Ugly Car, Pretty Girl, and Mr. Pridgen

As written for: Johnny M. Hunt

*"And He said to them, follow me
and I will make you fishers of men."*
Matthew 4:19, NASB

A delinquent youth meets the Savior, and becomes a leading soul-winner.

I was a seventeen-year-old ne'er-do-well that *summer of the ugly car.* A high-school dropout, teenage alcoholic, and habitual gambler, I was living my "lofty" life's goal—managing the local poolroom. I'd hung out there ever since I was able to come up with a forged ID the year I turned fourteen.

My first car was a beat-up 13-year-old Chevrolet. That car was *so ugly* I dared not be seen in it. It was so bad I asked my friend Dave to drive me home every day after work.

One day Dave said, "I'm kind of in a hurry today, John. Do you mind if I let you off at Carolina Beach Road? You could cut right through to your apartments." I told him I didn't mind, so he let me off, and I began walking toward home.

Just as I was about to cut through to the apartments—at 319 Bordeaux Avenue—I spotted a cute little girl about 5'2" outside her house, twirling a baton. The closer I got, the prettier she looked.

The next day, I decided it was silly for Dave to go so far out of his way just to take me home! "Why don't you just let me off at Bordeaux Avenue?"

From then on, he dropped me off at Bordeaux Avenue and I walked by that house. I wasn't even a Christian yet, but I remember praying, *If there is a God in Heaven, please let her be out there!* And sure enough, every day she would be outside, twirling her baton.

That cute little 5'2" baton twirler named Janet became my bride six months later. And what I didn't know at the time was that every day when she was outside twirling her baton, she was really waiting for me to walk by!

It's a wonder Janet ever got her parents' permission to marry me because of my bad habits. And sure enough, our marriage hit serious snags right away.

My downward spiral had started early. My Mom worked two jobs to provide for me and my four brothers and sisters. As the youngest, growing up with little adult supervision, I found it easy to get into trouble.

The government housing project where we lived had a community center and on weekend evenings, all the older guys would go up to the dance. I thought, *Boy, they are so cool!* My buddies and I began slipping into the bushes behind the building where they hid their whiskey; and at the age of eleven, I experienced what it meant to be drunk. By thirteen, I was an alcoholic.

At fourteen, I found a driver's license, used it illegally to "prove" I was sixteen, and became a regular, hanging out at the poolroom.

Every morning, Mom gave me lunch money for school. I'd walk straight to the poolroom and ask: "How long can I play for ninety cents?" For five years of my life, I played pool—sometimes for as long as eight hours a day. All the while, with a cigarette dangling from my lips, I drank, cursed, and gambled—gambled for large sums of money.

The first thing I did when I actually *turned* sixteen was to get my own driver's license. The second thing was quit school. Right away, the poolroom owner hired me as manager, which meant I spent most of my days *and* evenings there.

My lifestyle flirted with self-destruction. One night, in a borrowed car, I drove some buddies to a drive-in. Drinking heavily, we got into a scuffle that didn't go our way. I went home with one of my friends and got a shotgun, then headed back to the drive-in with every intention of killing the guy who I felt had done me wrong.

On the way there, I ran off the right side of the road. When I jerked the wheel back, the car went into a spin across the median. When we finally stopped, the car was upside down, facing the traffic. I was hanging out of the car, having been dragged down the road.

That escapade netted me a trip to the hospital, a night in jail, and a very angry owner of the car I had totaled.

After Jan and I married, I *tried* to do better, even worked an extra part-time job at a hardware store. But I always slipped back into my old ways.

Now, Janet began talking about our need for church. About every two months, on Saturday night she would ask me, "Can we go to church tomorrow?"

"Well," I would say, "let's wait and see in the morning." But in the morning, I would act like I was so tired I couldn't get out of bed.

Then N. W. Pridgen began coming by the hardware store. Mr. Pridgen never left without saying: "You know, Johnny, I wish you would come to church with me sometime." And I always made some excuse.

Mr. Pridgen's message began to change. One day he said, "Johnny, do you know an old boy that hangs around the poolroom by the name of Dan Tritt?"

"Yeah, I know Dan."

"Did you hear what happened to him last week?"

"No, I haven't seen him lately."

"Well," he said, "Dan got saved and Jesus changed his life."

Now I had never read a Bible verse and didn't know what it meant to get "saved". I thought people simply decided whether or not to be religious, and I had chosen not to be.

But let me tell you about Dan. At a Saturday night party, Dan had stood out in front of the poolroom, shaking his fist at the sky and saying, "If there's a God in Heaven, strike me dead!" And now I'm hearing that Dan is going to church and that God has changed his life!

Week after week, N. W. Pridgen came in, often with a report that Jesus had changed the life of yet another "good ole boy". And always he said, "Well, you know what I'm going to ask you, don't you?" And I sure did. I had heard it so many times it sounded like a recording on Dial-A-Devotion!

Finally, I told my wife, "If you're going to keep hounding me about church, let's just get up and go to the little church down the street where N. W. Pridgen goes."

After attending for several weeks, I began to feel pretty good about myself. Nothing had changed in the way I lived, but after all, I was in church now.

Then something began to happen to me. I would go to church and everything was fine so long as the sermon was being preached or somebody was singing. But then the preacher would say: "We're going to stand together and sing an invitation hymn." And I would begin to weep.

It embarrassed me, a big shot who hung around the poolroom—*crying!*   While the others bowed their heads in prayer, I'd ease out a handkerchief and erase those tears.

One cold Sunday morning in January, my wife and I were sitting in church, close to the back as usual, when they began to sing:

"Just as I am without one plea,

And that thou bidst me come to thee.

O Lamb of God, I come!"

This time Jan caught me weeping. "Are you alright?" she asked.

"Yes, I'm fine."

"Well, then, why are you crying?"

I just told her to "shut up." I didn't know what was happening to me or how to answer her.

Then the preacher, just before the closing prayer, said, "There's a young man here, and God's dealing with him. Let's just pray that God will bring him back tonight and save him."

After lunch that day, I didn't go to the drag strip where on Sunday afternoons I usually raced my red '67 GTO. I told Janet, "Why don't we hang around the house and go back to church tonight?"

Janet could hardly believe it. "You want to go back to church *tonight?*"

"Yeah, you know the preacher was talking about me this morning."

"Oh, Johnny, he wasn't talking about you! There were 300 people in church."

I knew better. "Janet, you know I've tried to clean up my act but failed." She nodded. "Well, if Jesus Christ can change my life, He's welcome to it."

"It's true, Johnny. He *can* change your life, make you a *new person*—that's why they sometimes call being 'saved', being 'born again.'"

7

Janet added, "Johnny, there's something I never shared with you. Before we started dating, I accepted Jesus and was saved."

"*You're saved*?" I was impressed. "Well then, since you're saved, I want you to do me a favor. I want to go to church tonight and when the invitation is given, I want you to go down and tell that preacher that *I* want to be saved!"

"No!"

"Come on! You know how timid and shy I am! I am not going to walk that aisle in front of all those people. I just can't do it. I'm too scared! Just go on down and tell him."

"No, *you've* got to go tell him yourself."

It came time to leave for church. "Listen, Janet, why don't we go down *together;* and you tell him I want to get saved?"

"No, Johnny, this is something you'll have to do on your own."

"OK," I said, taking a deep breath, "I'm gonna' do it. But Janet," I cautioned, "if Jesus doesn't change my life, I'll be the same old me tomorrow—I'll still be cussin' and drinking just like always. So I don't want you to bug me."

I sat there during that whole service, my mind consumed by the fact that when the invitation was given, I would be going forward to trust my life to Jesus Christ. When the singing started, I said, "Now, Jan?"

She said, "Now."

I went down front and told the preacher: "I want to give my heart and life to Jesus."

And that night, January 7, 1973, *Jesus changed my life!*

Word spread around town, "Have you heard about Johnny? He's got religion and now he can't drink and gamble anymore."

To which I explained, "No, I didn't get religion. I got *saved!* Jesus Christ changed my life! I don't drink and gamble anymore because I don't *want to.* Jesus changed my want to's."

8

I went to all my old haunts, sharing the Good News. I told people that what Jesus did for me, He would do for them. After I told the poolroom owner, he and his wife both got saved. Next day, he hung a sign on the front door "GONE OUT OF BUSINESS."

At the saloon, the manager, Roy Burch, was playing with a cap pistol. I said, "Roy, I just want to tell you the reason I haven't been coming down on weekends. Jesus changed my life! And Roy, I don't drink anymore; I don't cuss anymore; I quit smoking—He's just changed my life. Man, I'm living for Jesus!" And as I was sharing my experience with him, Roy laid that little toy pistol against his cheek and caught the tears that were falling from his eyes into the barrel of the gun.

Everywhere I went I told people that Jesus had changed my life. One day a skeptic, knowing my sordid past, asked: "Well, Johnny, what are you going to do now that you're saved and going to heaven?"

The answer came easy, "Take as many people with me as I can."

Now, twenty-six years later, my mission remains the same. I continue to tell everyone who will listen, "If Jesus could get me from the poolroom to the pulpit, He can change *your* life, too! Jesus is in the life-changing business!"

All the while my heart is adding, *Thank you, Lord, for rescuing this wayward son.*

Thank you for that ugly car, that pretty girl, and for Mr. Pridgen.

AUTHOR'S NOTE: Since December 1, 1986, Dr. Johnny M. Hunt has been Senior Pastor of rapidly growing First Baptist Church, Woodstock, Georgia.

NOTE: Names of some people and places changed to protect privacy.

By Way of Hope

As written for: Gene Beckstein

*"When Christ came into my life, I came about
like a well-handled ship."*
Robert Louis Stevenson

A teen-aged gang member finds Christ,
then devotes his life to helping
other kids in trouble.

The possibility never entered my mind that someday I would
be a teacher. In fact, the possibility was slim that someday
I would amount to *anything* worthwhile.

Born in the tenements of Buffalo, New York, I grew up
with no hope of better days. Violence there was a way of life.
When I was eight, the thunder of gunshots woke me. Looking
out the window, I saw a man die in the glare of a streetlight.
Oddly, it didn't seem that unusual.

We knew little of law and order. Even in our apartment,
brawls often erupted.

Our dad was a part-time prizefighter and a full-time
alcoholic. Combined with seven brothers, that made for a real
physical family. Following the tradition, at thirteen I beat up a
guy and spent eighteen months in a training school.

After serving my sentence, I rejoined my street buddies stealing hubcaps—and anything else we could find. Later, many of them either died in jail or from alcohol and drug abuse, products of an impoverished neighborhood that knew only hopelessness and despair.

Somehow I scraped by in high school. Then, after trying a few no-future jobs, I joined the Marine Corps. Four years of military service opened a new door for me. For the first time, I learned that there *was* a life beyond the ghetto. But that life required education. The G.I. Bill paid tuition for veterans and I accepted—my one-way ticket out of the slums by way of New York University.

I was a twenty-nine-year-old college freshman when a friend tricked me into going to Rochester to hear some guys sing. He didn't tell me the program would be in church—a place foreign to me. After the singing ended, a giant Purdue football player spoke. John Ducharte was six feet five, 255 pounds, and talked about being intimate with Jesus Christ.

Having played a little minor league baseball, I wanted to meet this dude—another athlete. After the program I walked up and shook John's hand. "Do you really believe all that rubbish?" I blurted out.

"I certainly do." John said, then added, "Do you have a minute?"

I followed him into a little room where he pulled out a couple of vinyl chairs. We sat down and he opened up his Bible. "Of course you know John 3:16, don't you?"

I lied and said yes. John Ducharte saw right through me and started reading that verse from the Gospel of John, "For God so loved the world, that He gave His only begotten Son, that whosoever believeth in Him should not perish, but have everlasting life" (John 3:16, KJV).

Then he read Romans 10:13, "For whosoever shall call upon the name of the Lord shall be saved" (Romans 10:13. KJV).

About then the door burst open and John's little four-year-old daughter swooped in. He didn't scold her for interrupting. Instead, he put his big arm around her and gave her a kiss. I was embarrassed. I had been taught that real men don't do stuff like that, especially in front of another man!

Before I could recover, John's wife rushed in. "I'm sorry, John," she began. But he just put his other arm around her and kissed *her*. I marveled at that scene, those two muscular arms around his loved ones. This man had something special, something I'd never seen before.

After the ladies left, John asked if we could pray, this time putting that huge arm around *my* shoulders. When this guy prayed, I glimpsed *God*! For the first time I saw that it was possible for ordinary people, even street people like me, to get to know God on a personal basis.

I cried.

"What's the matter, friend?" asked that gentle giant.

"I feel terribly far away from God," I managed.

He replied, "Good."

"What's good about that?"

"Because," he explained, "that's what Jesus is all about. He's the bridge to God. He's the mediator. You want God to come into your life—Jesus is the bridge. Would you like that?"

"I know I want whatever it is that you've got," I told him. Right on the spot I prayed to accept Jesus Christ into my life. And that life has never been the same.

Back home in Buffalo, I found an old, inner-city church where the people accepted me. Barely a month later, another door opened when I returned to Rochester, this time as athletic director at a youth camp.

Leading the Christian training there all week were young, just-starting-out Billy Graham, Cliff Barrows and George Beverly Shea. What a privilege for a brand-new believer, getting to work with those three. We were all put to the test, though, as rain played havoc with our schedule. I grumbled because I couldn't lead the outside activities I had planned; the youth were boisterous with no way to work off excess energy. Yet the Graham team remained calm and patient. I learned much from their worship sessions. I learned even more from their actions.

I could hardly wait to tell others the good news of Jesus. My opportunity came soon thereafter when I landed a part-time job at a Buffalo radio station. Each day I did ten minutes of news, often bad news. Then—with a quartet standing by ready to sing gospel songs or someone to give a Christian testimony—I'd say, "But hang on, we've got some 'Good News at Noon!'"

After college, I migrated southward and devoted the next thirty-seven years as a public school teacher, administrator and counselor. I coached high school baseball, basketball, and soccer. Often, while working with students—some in trouble with the law or the school—I called upon the patience Billy Graham taught me years earlier. And I called upon the memories of my ghetto days—the anger, the frustration.... Most of those young people needed to know God's love just as I did.

I retired in Gainesville, Georgia, and returned to the ghetto. This time, however, I went to help *others* find a way out. My wife, Margie, and I sold our home across town and moved into a little house next-door to the Melrose Housing Project so that we could be accessible to the people.

When I decided to start a feeding program at Melrose, Margie made the meatloaf, a neighbor furnished green beans and cornbread, and we put out the word: "Anybody hungry is invited to lunch." So it was that "Good News at Noon" was reborn.

I began working with all age groups, facing their many needs: countless hungry and homeless, gang-related trouble, drug and alcohol addiction, AIDS, frightened children who endure family strife. I saw again that insidious problem that prevails among those born into poverty, a problem I knew only too well—*hopelessness.*

13

I particularly wanted to reach the children, to somehow build self-esteem in them. I *know* how that child feels who gets on the school bus with not so much as a pencil, only to have to compete all day with children who sport shiny new lunch boxes. Remembering how John Ducharte helped change my life by telling me of God's love, I wanted to do the same for these children and their families.

Gradually, surprisingly, volunteers began to appear. Today, fifteen years later, they number in the hundreds—professionals and lay people, civic clubs and churches. We receive no federal money. Instead, business groups organize fund-raising golf tournaments; schoolchildren collect canned goods; groups coming to serve meals bring the food with them; retired physicians contribute their time, skills, even equipment. All desire to share the Good News: The Gospel of Jesus Christ.

Good News at Noon now feeds hundreds every day, provides a homeless shelter, medical clinic and dental clinic. Volunteers teach, mentor, and counsel. Each person who receives physical or mental help receives spiritual help as well. We tell each one, "God loves you. God's love can give you hope—hope, and help, for a better life."

God is blessing. Many lives have been turned around—drug addicts rehabilitated, jobs regained, families restored, little children playing without fear.

These are proud people; they just need a little help, that's all. I try to serve them in a non-judgmental manner, because someone once saw some worth in me. Thank you, John Ducharte. And thank you Billy Graham, Cliff Barrows, and George Beverly Shea. Thank you for sharing with me—The Good News.

NOTE: Gene Beckstein, lovingly known as "Mr.B," and his "Good News at Noon" have practically become household names, and well-respected in Northeast Georgia.

Now eighty-three and recovering from a stroke, Mr. B. says, "Besides the early Christian training Billy Graham gave me, he continues to set an example. For in spite of advancing age and serious health problems, he just keeps going. And so do I." Both continue to minister in the name of Jesus Christ, planting seeds of faith—and hope—in yet another generation.

The Day Cheering Stopped

As written for: John C. Stewart

*Jesus said: "Whoever comes to me,
I will never drive away."*
John 6:37b, NIV

**A high school football star who loses
his college scholarship, and his hope,
goes on a self-destructive path
until Jesus sends help.**

It happened on a cold day in January, mid-way through my senior year in high school. I tossed my books into the locker and reached for my black and gold Cougar jacket. From down the corridor, a friend called out, "Good luck, Johnny. I hope you get the school you want."

Playing football meant more than a game to me. It was my *life.* So the world looked pretty wonderful as I headed up the hill toward the gym to learn which college wanted me on their team.

16

How I counted on the resulting scholarship—had for years! It held my only hope for higher education. My dad, an alcoholic, had left home long ago and Mom worked two jobs just to keep seven children fed. I held down part-time jobs to help out.

Still, I wasn't worried. I had the grades I needed. And ever since grammar school, I had lived and breathed football. It was my identity.

Growing up in a little southern town where football is king, my skills on the field made me a big man in the community as well as on campus. I pictured myself right up there on a pedestal.

And everybody pumped that ego. The local newspaper mentioned me in write-ups; at football games exuberant cheerleaders yelled out my name; people said things like, "You can do it, Johnny. You can go all the way to professional football!" I mean, that was heady stuff and I ate it up. It kind of made up for my not having a dad to encourage me along the way.

Hurrying to the gym that day, I recalled all those football games—and all those *injuries!* I never had let any of them slow me down for long—not the broken back, nor the messed up shoulders and knees…. I just gritted my teeth and played right through the agony. I *had* to.

And now came the reward. A good future would be worth the price I had paid. So with a confident grin on my face, I sprinted into Coach Stone's office.

Coach sat behind his desk, the papers from my file spread before him. Our three other coaches sat around the room. No doubt about it, this lineup signaled a momentous occasion.

"Have a seat, Johnny," Coach motioned to the chair beside his desk.

"Johnny," he started, "you've worked really hard. You've done a good job for us. A couple of colleges want to make you an offer."

17

Something about his tone made me nervous. I shifted my sitting position.

"But Johnny," he said, holding my medical records in his hands, "Doctor Kendley can't recommend you for college football. Johnny, one more bad hit and you could be paralyzed for life. We can't risk it."

A long silence followed. Then Coach Stone's eyes met mine. "I'm sorry, Johnny. There will be no scholarship."

No scholarship?! The blow hit me like a 300-pound linebacker slamming against my chest. Somehow I got out of that office. I could not understand that they were thinking of my welfare. Instead, in my mind a punching bag reverberated, *You're not good enough ... you're not good enough ... you're not good enough....*

For *me*, the cheering stopped. Without the cheering, I was nothing. And without college, I would *stay* a nothing.

After that, I just gave up. And in so doing, I lost my moorings.

At first, I settled for beer and marijuana. Soon I got into the hard stuff: acid, PCP, heroin, cocaine—I tried them all. By the time graduation rolled around, I wondered how I would even make it through the ceremonies.

Several older friends tried to talk to me about God. Yet even though I had grown up in church, had even served as an altar boy, I couldn't grasp the fact that God had anything to do with my present problems.

A couple of buddies and I decided to hit the road. We had no money and no goal. Along the way, we got into stealing gas to keep us going. When we got hungry enough, we picked up some odd jobs. No matter how little food we had, we always managed somehow to get more drugs.

My anger continued to fester. It wasn't long until I got into a bad fight and landed in jail thousands of miles from home. It caused me to take a good look at myself and see how low I had sunk. "God," I prayed for the first time in years, "please help me. I'm lost and I can't find my way back."

I didn't hear an immediate answer. Nor did I clean up my act. We *did* head toward home but the old car had had enough. It quit.

I went into a garage, hoping to get some cheap parts. *Maybe I can patch her up enough to get us home.* I was tired, hungry, dirty—and very much under the influence. Yet a man there extended a hand of friendship. Even took us to supper.

After we were fed, Mr. Brown called me aside, "Son," he said, "you don't have to live like this. You can be somebody if only you'll try. God will help you. Remember, He loves you. And so do I."

I was buffaloed. He really seemed to care about me. And he called me "son." It had been a long, long time since a man called me "son."

That night, in my sleeping bag, I gazed up at the star-filled Texas night. The sky looked so close, I thought maybe I could reach up and touch it. And once again, I tried to pray. "Lord, I am *so* tired. If you'll have me, I'm ready to come back to you."

In my heart, I heard Him answer, "I'm here. Come on back, son. I'm here." He called me "son," just like Mr. Brown did! I liked that.

On the road again, I got to thinking, *If Mr. Brown, a complete stranger, thinks I can make something of myself, m*aybe I *can.*

I didn't straighten out all at once. But at least I started trying. And God kept sending people to help me. Like Susan. In September, this cute young thing—a casual friend from high school—came up to me at a football game, of all places. She kissed me on the cheek, "Welcome home, Johnny."

The day she said, "Johnny, if you keep doing drugs, I can't date you anymore," is the day I quit them for good.

Susan and I married and today have three beautiful children. We're active in our local church and operate a successful business. I can tell you the respect of my community means the world to me.

All these years later, I still can feel the sting of that day when the cheering stopped. The hurt doesn't linger though as I've learned I can live without the cheers. After all, I have a caring heavenly Father who calls me "son."

Which reminds me, I *do* have a cheering section—a heavenly one. Check out this Bible verse I discovered: "... there is rejoicing in the presence of the angels of God over one sinner who repents" (Luke 15:10, NIV).

How about that? Angels! Cheering for *me*!

I like that.

⚓

NOTE: Names of persons and school colors changed.

Rickey's Perfect Gift

As written for: Karen Peck

"Rest in the Lord, and wait patiently for Him."
Psalm 37:7a, KJV

Gospel Music Group *Karen Peck and New River*—and the love story that made it all possible.

All appeared routine that Sunday morning in South Carolina. For *me*, though, on that day—*everything* changed.

In the parking lot of the church where we were to sing, I sat in our tour bus with the rest of *The Rex Nelon Singers*, awaiting the time for our entrance. Through the tinted windows, watching the Moms and Dads—hand in hand with their children—jostling up the front steps of the sanctuary, I felt a twinge of envy. *Why can't that be me, Lord?*

Even as those thoughts surfaced, I felt guilty. *How can I be so greedy,* I scolded myself, *after all the good things the Lord has done for me? Haven't I been living my dream the past five years, singing professionally with a top-rated gospel group?*

Still, I couldn't stop my longings. Ever since I turned twenty-five the week before, I'd been thinking, *Something's not right here. I have the career I've always wanted—but*

21

something's missing. Now—the light dawned. *My own little family. That's what I yearn for._*

Until then, singing had been my life. When I was just three, Mama and Daddy would stand me up on a chair and get me to sing. Soon I was singing in churches—touching people's hearts with the gospel of Jesus Christ.

By high school, I was singing with local groups. We even got to front for *The Rex Nelon Singers* when they performed in our hometown, a particular thrill since I had kept their picture tacked up on my bedroom wall for years. Every night, I prayed, "Lord, please let me sing with this group someday."

His answer kept coming back, "Wait."

With no career offer in sight, I started college. But patience never was one of my strong points. Almost every day I cried, "Lord, I want so badly to sing."

Silence.

Two years later, to my great delight, a rainbow broke through the clouds. Rex Nelon himself called me. He reported *Uncle Alf and the LeFevres* were regrouping and needed a girl singer. Would I be interested?

"Oh, yes!" I fairly shouted into the phone. I gained valuable experience working with Uncle Alf.

The following year, Rex Nelon called again. This time *he* had a vacancy and I joined up with *The Nelons.* The group picture hanging by my bed back home *now* included *me!* We traveled all over the United States and Canada and to the Bahamas, sharing God's love through our singing. At last, I was living my dream!

Now, as ridiculous as it sounds, when I realized I was a quarter of a century old and not married, I went into total depression—depression which I could not shake. I felt my depression showed a complete lack of trust in God's plan for my life. Yet, my heart's desire was to trust Him, implicitly.

One happy day the Lord spoke to that heart. "Karen, I have it all under control, don't worry about it." The depression lifted and my usual effervescence returned. I surmised that since we were on tour 280 days a year, God likely would line up another singer somewhere for me, or maybe a preacher. Who else would understand my need to minister in this way? And put up with the crazy schedule? *Grant me patience, Lord, while I wait.*

Meanwhile, along came Rickey Gooch. My sister's roommate kept talking about her stupendous hairstylist. One day, desperate for a haircut, I found his phone number and called. He didn't have an opening. I begged, "You've just got to help me. You've just got to do something with this hair." He kindly agreed to work me in.

My long blonde hair in a ponytail, no makeup, wearing old grey sweats, I bounced into his salon. I saw this handsome guy—great smile, soft hazel eyes. *Oh, no! So that's who they've been telling me about all these years.* I flirted with him, I'll admit it. But no response.

I even phoned next day. "Rickey, I just want you to know that I absolutely *love* my hair! You did so good on it." He said, "Thank you. I appreciate it." Nothing more! Talk about *Mr. Cool.*

A week later I needed hair spray. Naturally I went to Rickey's shop for it. I reached into my handbag for the $4.00 to pay him when something said, *Write a check with your phone number on it.*

It worked. He called that night and asked me out. On the date, we sat and talked. His sincere, quiet-spoken manner won me right away—as a *friend.* Soon he became my *very best* friend. I never tired of being around Rickey. When I was on tour—which was most of the time—I missed him terribly. I was so comfortable in our friendship, every now and then I reminded God I was still waiting for that husband He promised.

This pattern continued for three and a half years. It came as somewhat of a shock one day when I realized, *I love this guy.* I almost laughed, to think that God had put one over on me. For I knew with a certainty He had prepared us for each other. Rickey tells me he knew much earlier we had something special, but was giving me time. That's just the way he is—so considerate, so caring.

We were married May 5, 1989 with a beautiful church wedding. I couldn't have been happier. I had my career. And now my wonderful husband. All the while, there were those who predicted, "It'll never work, Karen, a traveling gospel singer married to a dedicated-to-his-work hair stylist. He'll make you come off the road. You'll see."

Nothing could be further from the truth. Never once did Rickey criticize me for being away so much. Never once did he indicate any resentment for my being in the limelight, getting lots of attention. Rickey's ego was secure. Besides being film-star good-looking and a superb hair stylist, he operated two successful businesses, plus had all sorts of hobbies and other interests one of which was learning to play guitar.

On the other hand, a few months after our wedding, the Lord started dealing with *me*. Maybe I needed to make some changes. I didn't want to listen. After ten years together on the road, the Nelons were almost like family. How could I leave them? Besides, I'd be giving up my dream.

But during the long hours of bus travel between singing engagements, my inner turmoil continued. After much struggle, I surrendered. "Lord, even though I want so much to be a singer and I truly believe that You have called me to do that, still I feel you're telling me that my first responsibility right now is to be a wife. And that's what I want to be."

That night, as I pulled my car into our driveway, Rickey bounded down the steps, two at a time. His enthusiastic embrace fortified me for what I must do. We carried my suitcases inside. "Just leave them here in the hall, Rickey," I said. "We need to talk."

In the living room, we sat on the couch and he took both my hands in his. "What is it? You look serious."

"Rickey," I began, "I feel in my heart it's time for me to come off the road. I want to start a family. And I know you do." Rickey nodded agreement. "Meanwhile, maybe I could form a little group of my own, just to sing in this area, on weekends."

Rickey put his arm around my shoulders and pulled me close. Without hesitation, he responded, "Karen, this is your decision. I'm not going to try to influence you. But, whatever you decide, just remember, I support you all the way."

We sat for some while, neither of us talking. All of a sudden, without the slightest fan-fare, my dear husband surprised me with a gift—a gift so perfect I could hardly believe it. "I'll tell you what," he announced as if it were the most natural thing in all the world, "if you form your own group, I'll go with you and play guitar."

"You'll do *what?*" I jumped to my feet, ecstatic. *My hair-stylist husband will play guitar?* "Honey, that would be great! Wow!" I was overjoyed. I never would have dreamed that the two of us would have a ministry together. Who but God could have orchestrated such a plan?

In reverence to that Holy Presence, I rejoined Rickey on the couch. We sat there a long while—my head on his shoulder—thinking, mulling, knowing down deep that we were on the verge of real change and many challenges. But with God's help, we would face them together.

I'm not sure just when our planning changed from the little local group to a full ministry including two additional singers, a five-piece band, and our own tour bus. It just evolved, almost as if an unseen hand were directing. Rickey came up with our name, *New River.* Producers from all over called, wanting to book us. *Lord, this is a big step. But you've brought us this far. I trust You to lead us every step of the way.*

And it *was* a big step. For one thing, I'd never talked on stage and now I was designated MC. Me, a petite blonde who spoke in High C! "No one is ever going to take me seriously." I was wrong.

The first major concert for *Karen Peck and New River* was in January 1991 at Georgia Mountain Center in Gainesville, Georgia, my hometown. Appearing with *Gold City Quartet*, we played to a packed house—close to 4000 people. And quiet, stay-in-the-background Rickey was not even nervous on stage. Between songs, when I turned and glanced at him and he smiled back, I was filled with happiness. That night, as I walked off the stage—hand in hand with Rickey—I felt, for the first time, *this isn't going to be small like I thought,. God is about to take us further than I ever dreamed.*

There was still something missing though, and God fixed that too. Our precious son, Matthew, was born September 12, 1992. Ten days later, with my Mom along to help out, we took Matthew with us on the bus to fill an engagement in Little Rock, Arkansas. Soon, we began introducing him to our audiences, and they loved it. While just learning to talk, he sang for them and before long he even played the violin on stage.

Then our beautiful little Kari Faith joined the family and adds her own special light to our lives. The two of them, and their singing, win hearts everywhere we go.

It is at such times that I am overwhelmed with being so blessed—*singing,* with my loved ones around me. It proves to me that God's plans are always better than my own. I hope I'll remember that and just trust Him the next time He says, "Wait."

For I know now, the answer will come in His perfect timing.

Just like Rickey's perfect gift.

This Marine's Wakeup Call

As written for: Joe H. Stargel

"Storms have a way of teaching what nothing else can."
—John Ortberg, "If You Want to Walk on Water"

The author's husband tells
his side of the story.

I don't have time for this, I fretted inwardly while checking into the hospital that wintry morning. *The City Council meets next week, my Marine Reservist duty weekend is coming up, and my desk at the office is piled high.*

Regardless, I followed the doctor's orders and next day found myself strapped down on a gurney in the surgery recovery room, invaded on all sides by needles and tubes, while a twelve-inch vertical incision on my abdomen—held together with wire stitches—dared me to move.

Hours later, after the attendants had wheeled me back to my room, I managed with great physical effort to ask my wife, Gloria, "What did they do?"

"They removed a large tumor," she answered, carefully avoiding the word *cancer.*

As she smoothed my brow with her fingertips, I drifted back into the anesthetized world from whence I'd come. I never pushed for details. I would learn soon enough the unspeakable agony—both physical and mental—of the months yet to follow.

The date: February 8,1973. The enemy? Reticulum cell sarcoma, a rare cancer of the lymph system, described as "somewhere between Hodgkin's Disease and Leukemia."

The prognosis? A five-percent chance of slowing the fast-multiplying cells.

Possibility for a cure? None.

Life expectancy? Between six weeks and six months.

I had joined the Marine Corps at age seventeen. Now at forty-five I was still an active reservist. Basic training had taught me how to defend myself against an enemy. But nothing had prepared me to fight this sneaky, insidious *thing* that had attacked my body. It soon became apparent: since the medical community had no answers, this would take spiritual warfare for which I felt woefully unprepared

Years earlier, when I was released from active duty with the Corps, I had plunged into finding work and trying to catch up on schooling I'd missed.

At the same time, Gloria and I were in love and married soon after she turned eighteen. The two of us had the same goals: a home and family. When our sons Randy and Rick were born, we felt we had finally realized our dream.

Somewhere in the process, though, my life got out of kilter. A workaholic and a loner, I devoted more and more of my time to getting further ahead: a hundred-mile commute at night for two law degrees; nine years on the city commission, two of those years as mayor; monthly weekend drills and a two-week camp every summer with the Marine Corps. Plus a full-time job as corporate counsel with a road construction firm.

My strivings left little time for my wife and children, or even for God. Still, I considered myself a loving husband, good father, and an acceptable Christian. Didn't I work twelve hours every day to provide for my family? Didn't I go to church most Sunday mornings? Wasn't that enough?

When cancer struck, reality struck as well. Almost without my realizing it, my family had changed—Randy now a college junior, Rick a high-school senior, Gloria a wife I hardly knew, and *me* lacking spiritual strength.

I began fighting cancer the only way I knew how: *Stay busy. Try not to think about it. Maybe it'll go away.*

Just home from the hospital, frail and fourteen pounds thinner, I told Gloria, "I want you to drive me to the City Commission meeting today."

"You can't be serious," she responded. "You're in no shape to go out. The temperature is below freezing and flu germs are everywhere. Please, don't go."

"If you won't drive me, I'll call the police chief to come get me."

The thought of a blue and white police car pulling into our driveway convinced her, especially with the possibility of red lights flashing on top the car. She reluctantly drove me to City Hall.

But my show of courage was only for the public. At home, full of fear and self-pity, I withdrew into my shell, allowing no one to get close, not even my family.

Three weeks after surgery the oncologist began chemotherapy that caused me indescribable nausea, extreme weakness, deep depression, and numbness in my fingers and toes. At times I could not walk through the house without holding onto a chair or the doorframe.

After I had survived the six-months-to-live estimate, the doctors administered cobalt treatments—maximum dosage radiation to my torso, front and back, a procedure fraught with peril as they attempted to kill the marauding cancerous cells without killing the patient. Again, nausea and depression overwhelmed.

Following that year of debilitating treatments, my oncologist adopted a "wait and see" policy. He offered no hope, however, for long-term remission. Living with a ticking time bomb, I bore the ever-present fear that the cancer would reactivate at any moment.

As months wore on, my "born-to-worry" wife began to wear a sort of peace on her countenance. A sort of "I know a secret" smile.

Finally, I could stand it no longer. I found her in the kitchen, peeling potatoes for a casserole. "How is it," I asked her, "that with my life in jeopardy, you can look so serene?"

"Because," she said, setting the pan of potatoes on a burner, "I believe God is going to heal you, just like He healed people in Bible days."

"How can you believe that?" I questioned, pulling up a chair to the table. "You heard what the doctor said."

"Because," she said, joining me. "I've been studying in the Bible about God's love for us, about His promises to us. I've been reading other inspirational books, books telling about modern-day miracles."

"So?" She had my undivided attention.

"So," she said, "I'm convinced God still heals today, just as He did in New Testament days. Joe, I feel in my heart, He is going to heal *you.*"

"Why didn't you tell me all this?" I asked as I picked up the newspaper that I had just laid down.

"Because you never talk to me," she came back. "What little time you are home, the newspaper or television comes first."

Ouch! A loner like me was never too receptive of heart-to-heart talks.

Following through on her belief, Gloria enlisted prayers for me from every interested person. She must have bombarded heaven's gates with prayer requests for my life.

Her optimism proved contagious. I sometimes felt more positive myself. And I began asking myself, "Just what *are* my priorities?"

It took time, but finally this Marine recognized his illness as one dynamite of a wake-up call—a heaven-played reveille, if you will. "Joe, my boy," the message reached me, "you've had it all backwards. As important and necessary as work is, a truly successful person puts God first, family second, and work last."

Some months later, it is a typical Sunday afternoon as I join Gloria in the den. "Honey," I interrupt her reading, "are you ready for our walk? We have enough time before church service."

Yep. This workaholic, with God's crucial help and his wife's faithful support, heard—and heeded—his wakeup call. Heard it loud and clear. *Take time to live.*

Important Editor's note: After the Stargels lived under the cloud of cancer for ten years, the oncologist said—in a tone of amazement— "Joe, I think we'll tell the computer you're well."

Once An Athlete ...

" ... but in your hearts be consecrated to Christ as Lord, and always be ready to make your defense to anyone who asks a reason for the hope you have."
1 Peter 3:15a, Williams New Testament

A Devotional

Danny, my friend's teenage son, phoned on a Tuesday evening just as I finished washing the dinner dishes. "Mrs. Stargel," he began, "can you speak to the next meeting of our Fellowship of Christian Athletes? We meet Friday morning at 7:45."

"This Friday?" I gulped, stalling for time, wondering if I could prepare something on such short notice. "At *7:45*, in the morning? Danny, some days I'm not even out of bed at 7:45!"

Meanwhile, my subconscious was running over the *real* reason I hesitated to say yes. I pictured my audience: fifty high school students, restless to get on with life. What could this grandmother possibly share that would hold their interest?

I understood, of course, Danny had asked me to speak because of my Christian writing, especially with the recent

32

publication of a book. Yet, how could I build a bridge across two generations? *Lord, help!*

Then, quicker than a computer chip, the Lord dropped into my remembrance a few choice thoughts. "Don't forget, Gloria, *you* are a Red Elephant, too, just like these young people. After all, you were captain of the girls' basketball team at this very school."

Yes, Sir, I acknowledged inwardly. *But that was a very long time ago.*

"Well, then," the inner Voice continued, "remember—more recently — your son played defensive tackle on the Red Elephant football team. That should give you some connection, make you feel more comfortable."

I felt a small surge of enthusiasm. *Yes, Sir, that's true.*

"And besides all that," the pep talk continued, "you're *still* an athlete. Don't you play tennis matches every week?"

Indeed, I mused, *I thoroughly enjoy my tennis.*

"Well," He said, throwing in the quarterback's winning call, "think about this: Because you are a Christian—and because you are an athlete—that makes you a *Christian Athlete*, just like these students. So what's to keep you from speaking to them?"

He now had my full attention. *Not a thing, Coach, Sir, Thank you, Sir.*

Into the phone I said, "Yes, Danny, I'll do it. Where do we meet?"

To my relief, the young students made me feel at home. We spoke the same language, after all. To borrow from the Marine Corps' famous slogan "Once a Marine ...," I learned that "Once an athlete, always an athlete."

Lord, Jesus, somebody today needs your message of hope. Help me always be willing to share the Good News.

To Alaska, With Love

As written for: Walter V. Ashworth

What is a Yielded Life?
A life which love has won,
And in surrender full, complete,
Lays all with gladness at the feet
Of God's most Holy Son.
—W.A.G.
The Best Loved Religious Poems

A father's winter of tragedy— and triumph—in Tyonek.

The year was 1941, and Alaska was still a territory—a forbidding land of frozen mystery.

While teaching school in Braymer, Missouri, I had accepted a government job to teach in the small remote village of Tyonek, just 350 miles from the Arctic Circle. My wife, Evelyn, though concerned about the isolation, had accepted the job there of postmistress.

So it was that August found us in Seattle laying in provisions from an endless government list, including two tons of groceries to carry us through our first year in the wilderness.

On September 1, we put little two-year-old Billy Bob into his bright orange life jacket and boarded the *S.S. Baranoff* sailing north to Alaska. Ten days later, while darkness fast closed in on us, we took a small mail boat the 60 miles across Cook's Inlet to our destination. Never shall I forget that night.

The Tyonek villagers—Indians, Eskimos and Aleuts—had lit every lamp in our tiny house perched 90 feet above us on a bluff. As the mail boat pulled into Tyonek's harbor, the entire village stood waiting, waves breaking at their feet.

Since violent tidal surges of over 30 feet prevented the construction of a dock, we had to anchor 250 yards from shore. Dories came out to meet us and ferried us and our possessions ashore. For the last few yards the villagers *carried* us so we wouldn't get wet.

Finally everything was lying in great heaps against the bluff. I looked nervously at the encroaching tide—wavelets beginning to lap at the bottom crates. The villagers seemed not to notice and were chattering in Tlingit, a language so strange that I wondered if I'd ever grasp even its barest essences.

As dusk thickened, I could barely make out the dim outline of our provisions. Substantial as they were, they seemed totally inadequate to sustain us in this forsaken land. I began to shiver. Evelyn turned to me and asked in a trembling voice, "Walter, do you think we've done the right thing?"

We soon were so busy we didn't have time to wonder. Besides teaching eight elementary grades for the 40 village children, I operated a government radio communication system, giving a series of daily weather reports to Anchorage. I managed the community store and monitored the health of the reservation's population. I also tagged all the furs and recorded all the salmon taken in the region.

In addition to serving as postmistress Evelyn taught the women sewing, basket weaving, cooking and child care. Our small white frame house bustled with activity.

As harried as we were by our responsibilities, we took delight in how well little Billy Bob was getting on. He loved his new friends, and they reciprocated, calling him their "little white angel."

Each evening the little fellow watched the Aurora Borealis—his face the picture of joy under the Northern Lights. He was fascinated at how fireweed turned the countryside into a sea of crimson come fall, and how, soon after, it became pristine white in a feathery blanket of snow. Gradually we began to feel at home in this strange, awe-inspiring land. We began to view it through Billy Bob's entranced eyes.

This was just as well since, by November, Cook's Inlet was clogged with icebergs as big as houses, and boats no longer reached us. Even our radio conked out so that we were completely isolated.

One evening in the second week of November, Evelyn put Billy Bob to bed early. He had suffered a light cold for two days and then became hoarse that afternoon. He had no fever when we put him to bed, but he began coughing in the night. Ordinarily I would have radioed our doctor in Anchorage for advice, but the radio was still out.

As the night wore on Billy Bob's breathing became more and more labored. Evelyn and I tried frantically to help him as he struggled for breath. His heart was beating heavily and then grew irregular.

That morning, at 8:10 AM, the unthinkable happened. Billy Bob died. We never knew for sure whether it was pneumonia or membranous croup. He was not quite three.

The villagers were very kind. They made Billy Bob a tiny casket and in the classroom, conducted a funeral service that the entire village attended.

Evelyn and I couldn't find it within ourselves to comfort one another. Over and over I said to her, "We have paid a terrible price for bringing Billy Bob to Alaska. When summer comes, we will leave here forever." Evelyn could only nod.

Numbly, we went about our duties but I felt as if we were slowly choking to death on our grief. I called on my faith in God ... and found it lacking.

Yet, in the depths of my brokenness, I knew Billy Bob had gone to heaven. *If we expect to join him there*, my schoolteacher's mind reasoned, *we need some preparation.*

I went to the storage room and rummaged through the crates. At the bottom of a box of books, I found it—the Bible that had been a wedding gift to Evelyn and me. There on my knees, I clasped it to my chest and felt a flicker of hope.

That evening at supper I asked Evelyn, "Do you think we might set aside a time each night to read a bit of Scripture? Maybe say a prayer together?"

So it happened that every night just before bedtime, we sat by the oil burning heater in the living room taking turns reading a chapter of the Bible. Often as we read we could hear icebergs grinding menacingly against one another in the frozen harbor. Once the sound would have haunted us.

But within the Bible we had found a safe haven with promises of God's love. Daily we clung to verses like: "He shall cover thee with His feathers, and under His wings shalt thou trust " (Psalm 91:4a, KJV).

One day in March, after a long, dark winter, Evelyn and I took advantage of a break in the weather and went snowshoeing on a dogsled trail. It was a Christmas-card scene—aspens and spruce draped in fresh-fallen snow with majestic mountains in the distance spiking into a bright blue sky.

Suddenly Evelyn called out, "Walter, look, this reminds me of flowers we had back home—we called them `birdie bills'!" There, pushing up through the ice alongside the path, was a brave little forget-me-not. Evelyn's eyes met mine and I saw

37

in her gaze a peace and reassurance that I could feel mirrored in my own.

One evening I noticed that we often began our sentences with, "*If* we stay in Alaska ..."

When Cook's Inlet eventually thawed, we accepted a new assignment—a vocational boarding school in Eklutna, just north of Anchorage.

On May 1, as we boarded the mail boat to take us there, an image flashed in my mind—an image of Billy Bob, his face lit with the enchantment of the Northern Lights. That's the way I would remember him.

Finally I had accepted Billy Bob's life, short as it was, not as a tragedy, but as a gift.

AUTHOR'S NOTE: Walter Ashworth devoted the rest of his ninety-four years of life to serving his Lord. His good deeds were many. In his own words: "Life never again caught me without the Bible, either in my hands—or in my heart. Its teachings have guided me daily, through other tragedies—other triumphs. The greatest triumph, though, is yet to come. For by faith, I expect someday to live with Jesus. And with a little fellow named Billy Bob."

On February 17, 2003, Walter Ashworth received his reward when God called him home.

CHAPTER 2

Jesus, Our Lighthouse

Heeding His Guidance and Warnings

Jesus Saviour, pilot me,
Over life's tempestuous sea;
Unknown waves before me roll,
Hiding rock and treacherous shoal;
Chart and compass came from Thee:
Jesus Saviour, pilot me.

Edward Hopper, 1818-1888
John E. Gould 1822-1875
"Jesus, Savior, Pilot Me"

Harmony Restored

As written for: Bill Gaither

*"The home is a lighthouse which has the lamp of God on
the table and the light of Christ in the window, to give
guidance to those who wander in darkness."*
— Henry Rische: *The Windows of Home*

**When a Peter Practical marries an Edith Ethereal, tension
often erupts—even between dedicated Christian couples like
this song-writing pair whose compositions have inspired
millions.**

"Bill, we're going to walk on down to the beach," my
wife's voice trailed over her shoulder as she headed out
the door of our vacation condominium with our daughters and
their children. "We don't want to miss it!"

"Okay," I answered from upstairs, knowing this occasion
was important to her. "I'm right behind you."

A rare break in our schedule that January had permitted
Gloria and me a few days with our family on the West Coast
of Florida. The night before, on our way to dinner, we had
noticed a particularly beautiful sky and decided to allow time
this evening to watch the sunset from the beach.

B-r-r-r-r-i-inng ... *This shouldn't take but a minute,* I rationalized as I picked up the phone and said hello. It was a man I had tried to reach early that morning, someone on his way out of the country and whom I needed to talk to about an upcoming television appearance.

Despite my trying to hurry things along, the call became involved. In the middle of the conversation, Gloria came in and gave me a look only a wife can give. "What are you doing? Why are you making that call now?"

I covered the phone. "I'm not *making* a call; I'm *taking* a call, and I needed to hear from this guy."

"Well, hurry up. We're going to miss the sunset."

By the time I joined Gloria on the beach, the sun was a sliver of orange on the horizon. It provided just enough light to see her angry shrug. Gloria is generally better than I at saying what she's thinking, and her thoughts were strong: "When are we going to learn this? How old do we have to be and how long do we have to be in this ministry before we realize that some things are more important than others?"

Ouch! As a musician, I just naturally *hear* harmony. It doubly troubled me, then, that in our otherwise melodious marriage, sometimes there crept in these sour notes. Worse, these sour notes were *mine*, brought on by my tendency to miss many of what Gloria calls "memory-making-moments."

Apparently, I now had given in to this tendency one time too many. My normally sweet, loving wife was more than a little upset with me.

This time, though, I felt unfairly chastised. "Gloria, I'm sorry, but there was no other time I could talk to the guy."

At that point she couldn't have cared less if the caller had been President of the United States. My thoughts went something like: *I am married to this brilliant person who, in my opinion, does not understand the practical things of life. How can my wife of more than twenty-five years be so immature that she can not take into account the busyness of my schedule? Some things you have to take care of when you can.* My resentment was clear. I did not react well.

Gloria reacted to my reaction, and though we should have known better, it was fifth grade revisited. Suffice it to say, ours was not a pleasant dinner. If palm trees swayed in the ocean breeze, we didn't see them.

I couldn't believe that Gloria could not understand how complicated our life was. Especially since she had been an active part of it all along—writing the lyrics to hundreds of the songs we had composed; traveling with me all over the country performing as part of the *Bill Gaither Trio*; plus trying to maintain a healthy home life for ourselves as well as for our three children, now grown up. Oh, and did I mention producing videos? I try to keep it as uncomplicated as possible, but sometimes I don't have a choice.

But Gloria feels that some things are sacred and should remain sacred. And watching the sunset with the person you love most in the world is more sacred than any business detail.

In my heart I knew she was right. Still, I was outraged that she couldn't see the much bigger world out there. Clearly, our relationship at that moment could use some fine-tuning.

Truth is, I spend a good portion of my energy on the practical responsibility of making a living and keeping a business going, just like many of my associates. It is an ongoing battle trying to balance both real worlds: the practical and the ethereal.

Gloria and I happen to be on the extreme ends of the practical/ethereal spectrum. In fact, a longtime friend has called us Peter Practical and Edith Ethereal. To use a biblical metaphor, she's the Mary—Mary who felt it most important to sit at the feet of Jesus. And I'm the Martha—Martha who rushed around trying to get all the work done and risked missing the opportunity of a lifetime.

Most of my life is made up of the Mary/Martha dilemma: balancing the practical with those intangible things that will

last forever. The Lord knows, together we have written enough
songs about it, trying to call people's attention to what real life
is all about. Songs like "We Have This Moment Today"—

Hold tight to the sound of the music of living,
Happy songs from the laughter of children at play;
Hold my hand as we run through the sweet, fragrant
    meadows,
Making memories of what was today.

Tiny voice that I hear is my little girl calling
For Daddy to hear just what she has to say;
My little son running there by the hillside
May never be quite like today.

Tender words, gentle touch, and a good cup of coffee,
And someone who loves me and wants me to stay;
Hold them near while they're here and don't wait for
    tomorrow
To look back and wish for today.

Take the blue of the sky and the green of the forest
And the gold and the brown of the freshly mown hay,
Add the pale shades of spring and the circus of autumn,
And weave you a lovely today.

We have this moment to hold in our hands
And to touch as it slips through our fingers like sand.
Yesterday's gone, and tomorrow may never come,
But we have this moment today.

That's hard to argue with. I can sing it every night and
sing it pretty convincingly. Then the phone says, "*I* need this
moment," and the family wants to see the sunset. Sometimes
everybody gets the message but me.

44

Ironically, sunset moments are important to my work. I have to experience that intangible to be able to express it musically, and, if I theorize without tasting, my creative juices dry up.

But growing up on a farm in Indiana, I've always felt a certain amount of guilt if I wasn't working—and working pretty hard—most of the time. Fighting not to become a slave to that at the expense of the intangibles is my on-going battle. Surely there is a happy medium somewhere—a balance. *I can conquer this thing*, I determined yet again, jaw set. *I know I can.*

Three years and several missed sunset-moments later, Gloria and I carved out some time to get away together, just the two of us. No friends, no family, just us.

On the plane bound for St. John's Island, I couldn't resist using the time to proofread the manuscript of my latest book. I caught myself when I came to the story about the missed sunset in Florida.

The manuscript fell to my lap as I leaned back against the headrest and closed my eyes. *Dear Lord, thanks for the reminder. It's clear now, Lord, I'll need your help on this.* I put the manuscript away, closed my briefcase, and covered Gloria's hand with mine.

Our vacation in the tropical paradise was filled with memory-making moments. Snorkeling, swimming, jogging, or just exploring the town.

Each night we sat on the beach and watched a spectacular sunset, marveling at the kaleidoscope of colors which God orchestrated. I felt so fortunate, so blessed to have Gloria's whole attention on that trip, and I know she felt the same. The swaying palms danced a delightful ballet to an ocean-breeze symphony.

Yet the real test came back home in Indiana. It was a Thursday afternoon. I had been out of town Monday, Tuesday and Wednesday, and was scheduled to leave again Friday. That left only this afternoon to return some important business calls, business that *needed* tending.

In the family room our three-year-old grandson, Jesse, was on the floor playing with a yellow toy—a bug figure of some sort. When he pressed down on it, the bug would jump and make a loud noise. I was standing close by as Jesse applied his weight to that gadget and released it. Being a good papaw, I acted startled, patted my chest and exclaimed, "Oh, Jesse, you scared me!"

Whereupon little Jesse giggled and of course, tried it again. With each jump of the strange yellow creature, my acting got better and better—*my* jumps higher and higher. Four times. Five times. By now Jesse was laughing uproariously. Deep, down belly laughs.

"I've got to go now, Jesse," and I headed for the bedroom to get my notes. Jesse followed me. "Do it again, Papaw," as he pressed down on the toy. *What to do? I need to make the calls. The clock is ticking ... I choose—I choose Jesse!* My acting became even more animated and Jesse's contagious laughter filled the house. Soon our son Benjy was standing in the doorway, cracking up with laughter at this strange behavior on the part of his father and his little nephew.

An hour and fifteen minutes later, the little guy was all played out. As I swooped him up in my arms, Jesse laid his contented head on my shoulder.

Did I ever make the phone calls? No. And probably there were people who did not understand why I didn't get back to them. I hope they'll forgive me. But the time had come to prioritize. And I wouldn't trade for anything that precious experience with my grandson, seeing him have such fun, hearing that sweet laugh.... And having my own son share the moment made it even more special.

I thought of how often my wife had prodded me to enjoy the sunset moments—to balance the tangibles with the intangibles of life. Now with my grandson in my arms, I headed back toward the kitchen where the tantalizing aroma of chicken baking signaled a mouth-watering meal in the making. "Let's go find Mamaw, Jesse."

I wanted to tell Jesse's mamaw, "I've still got lots to learn, Gloria, about this sunset business. But I'm getting there."

Oh, yes, my refilled spirit sang, relishing the refreshing harmony in our household. *With God's help—I'm getting there.*

Portions of this story are adapted from:
I Almost Missed the Sunset,
by Bill Gaither with Jerry Jenkins
Thomas Nelson Publishers
Copyright 1992 by William J. Gaither.
Used by permission.

"We Have This Moment Today,"
Words by Gloria Gaither
Music by William J. Gaither.
Copyright 1975 William J. Gaither
All rights reserved. Used by permission.

Images

"... that they which come in may see the light."
Luke 11:33b, KJV

A Devotional

"Let me tell you what happened last Sunday," my friend Barbara said. "During the morning worship service, the congregation knelt to pray. As I bowed my head, a brilliance caught my eye, causing me to glance at the diamond ring on my finger.

"As I did," she continued, "the miniature image of a young boy's face looked back at me from the stone! Startled, I glanced up to see the sun beaming at just the right angle to catch the boy's likeness from a stained-glass window—and cast it onto my ring!"

Barbara's sparkling little story set me thinking about reflections. Mine in particular. What kind of image do *I* give back? I recall an old saying, "You are the only Bible some people ever read." What does *my* life tell them about Jesus? About His love?

Wouldn't it be wonderful if we could live so close to Jesus, in constant fellowship with Him, as to cause His divine light to radiate from us? So that when others saw us, they would get

48

a glimpse of *Him*? I believe that's what He wants us to do. I believe He wants us to shine. I plan to try.

Lord, help me to absorb Your light so that I might illumine the way for others. Amen.

Back on Course

As written for: Oscar T. Cassity, Major,
U.S. Air Force, Retired

*"The breeze of divine grace is blowing upon us all.
But one needs to set the sail to feel this breeze of grace."*
— Ramakrishna

He had flown all over the world, but found renewed faith in his own back yard.

Early rays of sun pierced between the blinds to wake me that March morning. *That's it,* I told myself. *No more putting it off. Today the garage gets its long-overdue cleaning.*

Armed with trash bags and my second cup of coffee, I attacked the project full force. From the top shelf, years of accumulated dust greeted me as I pulled out a carton from the neglected back corner. *My military mementos!*

I set the box on my workbench and began digging out keepsakes of my twenty-one years as an Air Force pilot. There were yellowed newspaper clippings, commendation certificates, grainy photographs....

Reaching deeper, my hand closed over an old leather-framed poem. *"High Flight"*! I brushed debris off the now-peeling frame and stared a long moment at the poem. *This went with me all over the world—Europe, Asia, North and South Pole—in combat zones and on peaceful missions. Everywhere I flew!*

My mind now in another realm, I recited to myself the memorable words of John Gillespie Magee, Jr. By the time I got to the closing lines of "High Flight," his inspired poem had swept me back up into the clouds:

Up, up the long, delirious, burning blue
I've topped the windswept heights with easy grace
Where never lark, or even eagle flew.
And, while with silent, lifting mind I've trod
The high untrespassed sanctity of space,
Put out my hand, and touched the face of God.

I pulled up a stool and sat there some while, basking in the moment—then wondering what had gone wrong. I had felt so close to God in those Air Force days. He had brought me through many dangerous moments. But why didn't I still sense His presence? Had I packed away my faith with my military memories?

A few months later, those questions still unanswered, I got on my lawn tractor to explore the wooded area behind my place, a tract of land apparently undisturbed for years.

To my surprise, about a fourth of a mile into tangled brush, I came upon a small cemetery, long abandoned. Carefully, I picked a path among the worn stones, finding few readable markers. One was for a little two-year-old girl who died in 1831. I felt strangely moved. There was a reverence there akin to that in a magnificent European cathedral. *The same reverence I used to feel when flying high in the clouds.*

I moved over to an ancient oak and sat on the ground, leaning back against the guardian tree. Awed by God's presence, I must have stayed there for more than an hour, mesmerized as shafts of sunlight and glimpses of brilliant blue sky filtered through low-hanging leaves, the whole effect that of a serene stained-glass setting.

I came away from that sacred place, my faith strengthened with a new awareness. God hadn't left me. It was *I* who had drifted off course.

And I know now: Even with both feet on the ground, my spirit still can soar—soar "where never lark, or even eagle flew...."

AUTHORS NOTE: Shortly after Major Cassity discovered the little cemetery, he saved it from almost certain desecration, maybe even destruction. A housing developer was clearing for a golf course adjacent to the Major's property. One day, Cassity looked out just in time to spot a bulldozer digging up trees and everything else in its path. It was headed straight for the hidden burial plot. Major Cassity reached the driver just in time. The sacred ground is now designated a protected area.

Sometimes It Takes a Lemon Pie

As written for: John Martin

*"If you want your neighbor to know
what Christ will do for him, let the neighbor see
what Christ has done for you."*
— *Houston [Texas]Times All-Church Press*

Things weren't going well in dealing with their new neighbors.

I was peering out the window when my wife, Grace, dashed into the kitchen with a bag of groceries. "Just in time," she said, out of breath. "It's beginning to rain and a downpour definitely is on the way."

Grace began unpacking the groceries and had just put a bag of lemons in the refrigerator when I called over my shoulder, "Grace, you have got to come over here and see this." Her gaze followed my pointing finger to the rain-coated female figure hard at work on the small hill behind our house.

"Whatever is she *doing*?" Grace asked.

"Mrs. Clark is piling rocks in my drainage ditch!" The hair on the back of my neck began to bristle.

"Why in the world would she do *that?*"

"I don't know," I told her, my temperature rising by the moment. "But I do know those rocks will clog it up. All the rain water coming off that hill is going to wash right through our yard."

This was not the way I had wanted to start off in our new home. Having just moved in, I wanted to make a good impression, to be on friendly terms like in our old neighborhood. But I could see *this* next-door neighbor was going to make that very difficult.

Our property backed up to a public park on which the hill in question was located. A shallow drainage ditch ran on public property behind the Clark's house. I had consulted with the man in charge of the park for permission to extend the ditch behind our house as well. Thus it would catch the runoff from the hill and divert it to a vacant wooded area down the street.

The day following that rainy episode, I removed the rocks from my ditch. The moment my back was turned, Mrs. Clark put them back. *I see this is going to be covert warfare,* I told myself; being more rankled each time those rocks appeared in my drainage ditch.

Grace, meanwhile, was anything but happy over this territorial wrangling. "I don't like having neighbors angry at us," she moaned. "They're not even speaking when they drive by."

"Well, *she* started it," I shot back, sounding like a five-year-old. "She ought to leave my ditch alone."

So it went for several weeks, no one speaking, Mrs. Clark and me taking turns sneaking rocks in and out of the drainage ditch. By then, I did not even *want* to speak, certainly not speak anything pleasant.

One day I came through the kitchen to find Grace baking a lemon pie. "Who's sick?" I ventured my usual line. "Or dare I hope that pie is for *me?*"

"The pie is for the Clarks," she said. " I'm taking it over just as soon as the meringue browns."

"Why would you take them *anything?*" I came back, "after how spiteful she's been."

"Because," Grace said, "this whole thing has been eating at me, especially since last week when my study group read that Bible verse."

"What verse?" I questioned. *

"The one where Jesus says that if someone harbors ill will against me, even if it is not my fault, then I am required to try to make amends." Grace peeked into the oven allowing to escape the heady aroma of hot pastry. "The minute I heard that scripture," she said, "I knew I had to do something. But what?"

Grace retrieved from the oven a baked beauty, meringue standing at attention. "Yep, this is the answer," she said, proudly displaying the pie. "I knew it this morning when I saw the new bag of lemons in our refrigerator. I remembered how my grandmother was always baking something, aiming to 'brighten someone's day.' And her lemon meringue pie was a favorite!"

"It'll never work," I warned, heading outside.

I was on the riding mower cutting the back lawn when Grace came out the kitchen door, fresh-baked pie in hand. "What if she closes the door in your face?" I questioned.

"Then I will have fulfilled my duty," Grace said and off she marched across the sun-drenched yard. I just shook my head.

---

* "Therefore, if you are offering your gift at the altar and there remember that your brother has something against you, leave your gift there in front of the altar. First go and be reconciled to your brother; then come and offer your gift" (Matthew 5:23-24, NIV).

Not for one moment could I understand how my wife would lower herself like that.

I watched for her as I rode back and forth on the mower. Grace didn't return right away. The thought crossed my mind, *Should I go check on her?* I finished the mowing and still she was not back.

Sitting on the back stoop with two glasses of ice-cold lemonade, I waited. When Grace came around the corner of the house, she was humming a little tune. "What happened?" I wanted to know.

"Why they were just as nice as they could be. They invited me into the den where we had a nice visit."

She hesitated slightly, as if assessing the situation. "They seemed to truly appreciate the pie, although probably they *were* somewhat surprised.

"And speaking of being a little surprised," she said, changing the subject, "where did you get this wonderful lemonade?"

"I found a couple of lemons you left out and I made it myself," I shrugged. "I figured you'd be upset when you came back and this might cheer you up."

We let the matter of drainage-ditch problems drop for the time being. But even with Grace's glowing report, I was still skeptical of the whole scenario. *Do you suppose that sort of thing really works?* I asked myself. *Will her simple act of obedience to the scriptures actually change our neighbors' attitude?* It never occurred to me that *my* attitude could use a little adjustment.

I didn't have long to wait. Grace and I were working in the front yard a couple of days later when the Clarks drove by—and threw up their hands in friendly greeting! Grace couldn't wave fast enough. "Well, now, that's better," she said, a satisfied smile filling her face as she reached for a wayward weed behind the shrub border.

For the next couple of weeks, the weather was dry and the drainage war quiet. One morning, I answered the front door bell's ring to find Mr. Clark standing there, clutching a huge bag of something in his arms. "We're just back from vacation and bought these great-tasting apples on the way home," he said. "They're Rome Beauties! We thought you folks would enjoy some."

"I'm sure we will, "I stammered. "Thank you!"

I turned around to carry them to the kitchen and met Grace coming up the hall. "Look at these!" I gushed. "Would you ever have thought it?"

Grace just smiled.

"I was thinking," I said, placing the apples on the counter and feeling downright sheepish, "maybe it would have been more neighborly if I had discussed our mutual drainage problem with the Clarks at the beginning. Together, I'm sure we can work out a solution."

Grace gave me a warm hug. "And *I* was thinking," she said, examining one of the Rome Beauties. "How would *you* like a hot apple cobbler for dinner?"

"I'd love it," I answered, planting a quick kiss on her cheek. "And while you're baking, I think I'll go next door and mend a few fences, or in this case—drainage ditches."

I sauntered on out into the yard, pondering the recent series of events.

One thing I knew for sure: I had witnessed Bible truth in action. And I decided that what it takes—first of all—is a willing heart.

And, then—sometimes—it takes a lemon pie.

NOTE: Names of people and places changed to protect privacy.

Learning from Judy

As written for: Larry Burkett (1939-2003)
Founder, Christian Financial Concepts

"For the Lord is good and His love endures forever;
His faithfulness continues through all generations."
Psalm 100:5, NIV

A consultant in managing money God's Way shares insights learned from his wife.

After Judy and I married, I was so sure she would be a spendthrift, I sought to control all our finances. As you might imagine, we argued—a lot. Not too surprising, I guess, when you consider that money problems are listed more than any other factor, including infidelity, as a major cause for divorce.

In our case, though, I became a Christian at age thirty-five and began to study the Bible. I had been told that God's Word offers practical wisdom for all of life. What gained my attention, however, were the many references to money—over 700 of them. That convinced me. God *cares* how we handle our money. And, He wants to teach us the best way to do that.

58

My study and application of Biblical guidelines restored peace to our home. In fact, I was so impressed I became a consultant in order to help others. Here are just a few of the principles God lays out. They can keep money matters from marring a marriage.

1. Appreciate Differences

"An excellent wife, who can find? She is far more precious than jewels. The heart of her husband trusts in her, and he will have no lack of gain" (Proverbs 31:10-11, ESV).

When we first married, I would tell Judy, "I'm basically a frugal person," especially when she mentioned buying clothes. Once, a couple of years later, she said, "You're basically a cheap person and there's a difference." I now realize that God put Judy in my life to help provide the balance I need. Without her I would never buy furniture, and without me she would never change the oil in the car.

A God-based marriage is two people willing to totally merge their lives as partners to utilize their strengths. That's called balance, and that's what a marriage should be. In the area of finance, balance is especially critical. God *uses* opposites in a marriage—once we recognize that "different" does not mean "inferior."

2. Communicate, Negotiate

"... with all humility and gentleness, with patience, showing tolerance for one another in love," (Ephesians 4:2, (NASB).

When Ron's wife, Julie, called for an appointment, her voice held a sense of urgency. "Please help us! My husband borrowed money for an investment which failed. Now it looks like we'll lose our house!" Ron had ignored this requirement to communicate. Most women are excellent money managers, and it is quite possible that Julie's input would have helped keep her husband out of an unwise get-rich-quick scheme.

Communicating and planning are the keys to success. It's a matter of determining where we are financially, having a plan that is fair to both, and talking about it, regularly and calmly.

3. Practice Patience and Perseverance
"Trust in the Lord and do good; dwell in the land and cultivate faithfulness" (Psalms 37:3, NASB).

When Judy and I first started out, we did what many young couples do— achieve. I've seen this path get many into bankruptcy, divorce—or both. Fortunately, before *our* situation got out of hand, we learned to "cultivate faithfulness."

"Cultivating faithfulness" implies a sequence of time— planning, planting, nurturing—and any attempt to circumvent the process usually ends with one result: no harvest.

4. Determine to Learn
"The naïve believes everything, But the sensible man considers his steps" (Proverbs 14:15, NASB).

One afternoon, I received a call from a young man I'll call Lee who sounded very desperate. He said, "I have an urgent problem. My wife, Melody, has been arrested for writing a bad check, and they put her in jail!"

After we bailed her out, I asked Melody, "Why did you write a bad check? Did you do it purposely?"

"No", she said, "I don't understand it. I was sure I had enough money in my account to pay all my bills." Melody is but one of many who never learned to balance a checkbook. Yet, she is an intelligent woman with a graduate degree. There are many books, as well as people, that will teach you how to keep records, plan a budget, and make wise investments. By combining basic skills with God's principles, we stay out of trouble—with the law, as well as our spouse.

5. Strive for Contentment

"For I have learned to be content in whatever circumstances I am" (Philippians 4:11, NASB).

One of the most important things about financial management which God taught me concerns our need to stay out of debt. As a Christian, then, we never embarrass the Lord by not being able to repay.

I find I can best stay out of debt by heeding the above scripture—by learning to be content with what I have. Indeed, I have observed in talking with others that whether a person has $250 or $250,000, it always falls short unless that person adopts an attitude of contentment. If we don't settle early in our marriage that money is *never* going to make us happy, we'll spend our entire life chasing after the Joneses, only to discover that when we finally catch up with them, they have refinanced.

It all comes down to this: *God owns everything.* Therefore, we must manage all we have according to His rules. If we, as husband and wife, will do that, we will come out with a healthy, balanced marriage.

Thankfully, Judy and I learned early to live that truth.

God is good.

Trust Him.

Portions of this story were adapted from: *Answers to Your Family's Financial Questions* by Larry Burkett, ©1987 Focus on the Family. Used by permission of Judy Burkett and by Crown Financial Ministries.

My Sister, Queen Margaret

"To know one's self is the true; to strive with one's self is the good; to conquer one's self is the beautiful."
—Joseph Roux: "Meditations of a Parish Priest"

Love between sisters survives sibling rivalry.

A s Amtrak's, *The Crescent* lurched forward, I plopped into the first vacant space. I was feeling so self-sacrificing, traveling all day to Biloxi, Mississippi, for the Ms. Senior America Pageant. Presumably I was going to cheer on my sister Margaret, the reigning Ms. Senior Georgia. Now I couldn't help wondering if anyone would go to all this trouble for *me.*

While I adjusted the basic-burgundy seat, the remark of a new acquaintance needled me yet again. Earlier, at the state pageant, Margaret had just been crowned and I was meeting some of her friends. One of them remarked, "Do you get tired of being introduced as Margaret's sister?"

Do I? I asked myself. *And why do I have mixed feelings about taking this trip?*

One would think that by the time one qualifies as "senior," one wouldn't need to contend anymore with sibling rivalry.

Not that I don't have much to envy about my big sister. I harbor lifetime memories of Margaret in the spotlight. And me, watching from the wings. Still, Margaret and I have always been close. *Lord, I want to be truly happy for my sister. Help me to support her whole-heartedly.*

The train gathered speed while through the window I watched the backside of our home state slide by, small towns with their all-but-abandoned depots echoing an era past—a perfect backdrop to the black-and-white movie going on in my head, a collage of random remembrances.

Scene One shows little-girl Margaret standing on the piano bench. "Daddy's little blue-eyed Marge," our father brags as she sings and dances for any audience around. Margaret—with the sunny disposition and Daddy's Irish good looks.

During the time my bound-for-Mississippi train zoomed along the straight-aways, then snaked around the curves, the internal documentary revealed that the patterns for our lives—Margaret's and mine—were set early. *She* would be the fun-loving one, always "on stage"—singing, dancing, playing piano, wearing the current fashion, the more flamboyant the better.

I would be the practical one, the organizer—clipboard and whistle always ready. As for clothes—jeans and tennis shoes for me, please. Through the years, I knew better than to compete in *Margaret's* world. So I carved out one of my own with a respectable number of spotlight moments—academics, sports, leadership skills....

Even so, it didn't seem quite fair that Margaret never needed braces on her teeth, never had feet that hurt in pretty shoes, always could do her own hair … and fun to be around! To this day, the party can't begin until Margaret arrives.

Then there are her talents. Take her high-school graduation, for instance: I can see it plain as day. Margaret is on stage wearing the gorgeous dress Mother made for her—gold crepe with a long, fitted waist, covered buttons, and full skirt. Poised and sure, she sings to the wartime audience a heart-rending "My Buddy."

This prompts me to recall the disaster of talent night when *I* graduated. Possessing no talent, four of us girls decided to *harmonize* on a current ditty: "Cement Mixer." I don't think we made it past the second "cement mixer, putty, putty" before our quartet fell apart, laughing hysterically. I have no idea what I wore.

Funny, the things we remember, I pondered, watching kudzu hanging from pine trees grab for the train windows as we zipped past.

I think about how Margaret has *always* loved to perform. Barely in her teens, she lined up on our porch some little cousins and me, trying to teach us to tap dance. We were practicing the "Shuffle Off to Buffalo" when one cousin shuffled right off the porch.

There even was the circus phase. An uncle had an old white horse out on his farm. He and Margaret decided she would learn to dance ever so gracefully on the bare back of that horse. It's a wonder she didn't break something.

Later, during the war, she gathered a string band, a master of ceremonies, and together with a girl friend worked up a fine patriotic show—singing and dancing at the movie theatre between films. Mother made their costumes, and where was *I*? Turning pages for my best friend who played piano.

Margaret's showmanship and my "whatever" gave way to marriage, children, scout work, PTA … But as soon as time allowed, she became active in local theatre productions and with grooming young hopefuls for beauty pageants. While *I* became a writer and took up tennis.

On the train that day, my in-the-mind movie came to a screeching halt when *The Crescent* slowed, then came to a metal-on-metal stop, sparks flying.

At the Biloxi Grand Hotel, the atmosphere was electric. Elegantly gowned ladies rushed about, their crowns glistening, their sashes indicating over which state they reigned, each queen surrounded by an entourage of enthusiastic supporters.

Finals for the pageant were held in the Biloxi Grand Theatre. I went early to meet with Margaret's "back-up crew" who were distributing cardboard fans in the shape of a peach bearing her photograph and the caption: "Georgia Peach, Margaret Culberson, Dalton." We were instructed to wave them with gusto at appropriate times during Margaret's appearances on stage. *Now why didn't I think to get her something like that? When my book was published, Margaret surprised **me** with a huge stack of posters.*

I leafed through the program book that had photos of each State Queen. *Why didn't I think to purchase a page?* I lamented further. *Margaret set up all sorts of things for me—book signings, radio interviews, helped me prepare for television …*

One of her pages in the program book hit a nostalgic nerve—it featured a picture of Margaret as a beautiful young mother with her three little girls.

In my memory stirred a hazy scene from the past: I am not quite six. Painfully shy, it's my first day of school and Margaret is holding my hand, gently easing me into the classroom. She whispers in my ear, "Don't be afraid, Gloria. I'm right down the hall." And throughout the day, I catch glimpses of my big sister outside the door, checking to see if I'm okay.

I had wondered if anyone would go to any trouble for *me* when, in fact, Margaret already had, time after time. *Ever since we were children,* I realized with a start.

Figuring it's never too late to make amends, I determined that when the curtain went up on Margaret's segment, I would be the best fan waver in the crowd! And I was!

She performed beautifully, a rousing song and dance number. Later, even though she did not win the big title, being voted most photogenic was quite an honor.

On the train trip home, I thought again about that innocent question. *Tired of being introduced as Margaret's sister?* Not anymore. Instead, I consider it an honor. After all, I'm the only person in the whole world who holds the position of *Margaret's sister.*

I closed my eyes, the better to see. *Thank you, God, for that special closeness of sisters. It's a feeling of warmth and caring that transcends all time and space—and individual gifts. Even sibling rivalry and selfish oversights.*

Back at my desk, I click on the computer. I will give Margaret something that only I can give. A write-up, complete with glamour photo, in her hometown newspaper, *The Times*— in Gainesville, where I still live, and write.

I begin: "My Sister, Queen Margaret ..."

Lesson in Grace

As written for: Bob Christmas

*Jesus said: "My grace is sufficient for you,
for my power is made perfect in weakness."*
2 Corinthians 12:9, NIV

This football coach—and father—learns a lesson in grace.

It had rained all that day in Bedford County, Virginia, and the football field was one big mud puddle—enough to dampen anyone's spirits. As head football coach of Jefferson-Forrest High School with a Friday night homecoming game at stake, I was wound up tight. Our Cavaliers out on the field, meanwhile, seemed to have lost their focus. Especially my son Robby.

Tension had been building all year between Robby and me, ever since as a junior he had moved up to the varsity team. And since he played quarterback—the position I coached—I was plenty hard on him. I wanted my son to become a great football player. At the same time, I didn't want anyone to accuse me of playing favorites. So I came down heavy. Being a dutiful son, he never argued back. But often in the car or at home after practice, or after a game, a huge wall of silence went up between the two of us—a wall so thick it seemed impenetrable.

At tonight's game the band, in their red/white/black uniforms, struck up our school rallying song. The cheerleaders, waving red and white pompoms, tried valiantly to generate some enthusiasm in the soaked stands and on the soggy field.

I had Robby playing free safety and if I had told him once I had told him a hundred times, when playing free safety there is one thing you never do—"Never let the receiver behind you." The ball was put in play. Robby dropped back. But for some reason he hesitated, hesitated just long enough for the guy to get behind him. The ball went over Robby's head, and the receiver caught the pass. I was livid. From the sidelines I barked, "Robby, get over here!" Number 5 dragged himself off the field, looking like a puppy expecting a chewing out. "Stand right there," I scolded, "and don't move a muscle." The fact that I had humiliated my son—in front of his team, his peers, the whole crowd—never occurred to me. I was too busy trying to win a ballgame.

Another night, we were in an attacking scrimmage. I gave the guys the play and said, "I want you to hit this pattern." Robby dropped back but instead of going for the play as instructed, he threw a bad pass to the wrong person. I went nuts. I yelled out to him, "I told you to hit the drag! Why in the world didn't you hit the drag?"

I knew I was tough on Robby, but as the oldest of my six children and the first son to play football for me, I wanted him to be the best he could be. Yet, I couldn't seem to separate being his father from being his coach.

At home one night, I went into his room and found him crying. I sat beside him on the edge of his bed, a father now, not a coach. "What's the matter, son?"

The floodgates opened as he began to lists the hurts I had inflicted on him while playing football. "Dad, you make me the scapegoat. All the time."

"What do you mean?"

"There can be six of us talking while you want us to listen, yet it's always, 'Robby, get quiet.'" Then Robby added with emphasis, "And it isn't said with much grace or mercy."

He wasn't through. "You always put me down, Dad, if I make the slightest mistake. Sometimes, even when someone *else* makes a mistake. Yet when I do something right, you don't say a word. I feel like nothing I do is good enough for you."

"Robby, I am so sorry I've hurt you." By now, *I'm* almost in tears. My family is the most important thing in the world to me. I've always tried to be a good Christian influence on them. I didn't realize I had let football affect how I treated my own children.

"I'm beginning to see what happened," I confessed. "I have been so afraid someone would accuse me of favoritism, I went too far in the other direction. Besides that, I guess I hoped that by fussing at you, the others would know what not to do. That was totally unfair." I wrapped my arm around his drooping shoulders, "Will you please forgive me?"

"Dad, I *want* to be a good football player, as much as you want me to be."

"Yes, Robby, I know that. But because you are my son and I want the best *for* you, I expected perfection *from* you. That's too much to ask of anybody."

I did some serious praying that night, asking God to forgive me, too. *Help me, Lord, to be a father who encourages—not one who drives my child to despair.*

I'd like to say I changed overnight. But it took me the rest of Robby's junior year to learn to separate being his dad from being his coach. And truth is, I'm a tough coach. But I tried to be fair about it and stop using Robby as a scapegoat. Not always successfully, I'm afraid.

It didn't help our relationship when I blew it in a big way at the end-of-season football banquet for parents. At the podium,

I called out the names of all the players. "Did I leave anyone out?"

"Yes, your son." It was Robby.

Lord, I've failed again. And again, I had to ask Robby to forgive me.

Things weren't much better his senior year—a year that should have been special because now Robby was heir apparent to the star quarterback position. He had a great pre-season. But on the last play of our pre-first-game scrimmage, Robby, 5 feet 5 inches weighing 125 pounds, made a run down field and some pretty heavy guys piled on him. After they peeled off, he crawled out saying, "Dad, something's wrong with my neck. It hurts."

I insisted he get back in there and finish the possession. He did, then repeated, "Dad, I'm hurt."

"Ok." I said, "Go see the trainer."

The child's collarbone was broken. I had failed yet again. Big time.

We both were devastated. The doctor said Robby would be out of the game at least five weeks. It took eight. By then, he had lost his starting position as quarterback and was never able to regain it. When finally his injury allowed him to play again, I'd let him go in the game from time to time. But his season was ruined.

Upon graduation, our tiffs were farther apart since he no longer was playing football for me. However, while attending college, he began coaching with me. Even then, I would forget my professionalism with him from time to time. He learned to come over close and remind me with one word said in that certain tone, "Dad ..." I immediately knew I had again crossed the boundary.

Finally, I had the opportunity to clear the air between us. *I can't make up for all the slights and hurts I have inflicted in the past. But I'll do something I should have done all along.*

With both of us as coaches, we were at our first end-of-the-season banquet here at North Hall High School in Gainesville, Georgia. Guests came dressed in their Sunday best. Decorations with our school colors of green and white gave the dining hall a festive air. Balloons hung everywhere, crepe paper streamers were draped in strategic places, while on the table tiny green footballs perched at each plate and football helmets holding flower arrangements provided centerpieces. All honoring our Trojans who had just finished a winning season.

I took the microphone to introduce our coaches, who in turn would introduce each of their players. When it came Robby's turn, I told the group a little about how he had played for me. "He was a good player," I said, "but he had to put up with a lot from me. Many nights I had to come home and ask his forgiveness for treating him so unfairly. But he's forgiven me and we've moved on."

I finished with, "Now he's coaching for me, and I have to say, he is one of my best coaches." I turned to where he was sitting, "Robby, great job!"

Robby strode up and accepted my extended handshake. Then he had his own nonprofessional moment—he hugged his head coach. Beaming all the while, I hugged back. And the audience? The audience loved it and burst into enthusiastic applause. There may have even been a few moist eyes.

Soon after, my wife Peggy shared something Robby had recently told her. "Mom," he said, "the things I had to deal with while playing for Dad were difficult. He was hard on me; there were some harsh treatments that were not right. That's just true. But, Mom," he went on, "I'll take all that for the experience of playing for the best coach there is."

Thank you, Robby, for extending grace to me in the midst of all my humanness. By your example, I have learned a vital truth—one I needed to know. As humans with human weaknesses, we must be patient with each other just like our

Sweet Sixteen

As written for: Shelly Teems Johnson

"I have hidden your word in my heart that I might not sin against you."
Psalm 119:11, NIV

A rebellious teenager "comes home."

"Hurry and get dressed, Shelly," Mom's overly-cheerful voice penetrated the closed door to my room. "The sun's shining. Let's go riding!"

Mom knew good and well that I was on the phone with my boyfriend. The last thing in all the world I wanted to do on that Sunday afternoon was go horseback riding with my mother. Yet, I dared not argue back, not after our blow-up the night before. *I'm sixteen-years-old, for crying out loud!* I seethed. *Why can't she just stay out of my life?*

Sometimes, I *hated* my mother. I desperately wanted her to give me a little space. She sponsored my cheerleader squad. She came to every one of my volleyball and softball games. She even taught at my school. Wherever I went, she was there! As if that were not bad enough, she was always ordering me around. Even my friends commented about it.

When I was little, I *liked* it when Mom was protective, when she got involved in my activities. But now I wanted more independence, a chance to make my own mistakes.

Truth is, in spite of Mom's constant surveillance, I managed to break most of the rules at our private Christian school. And the more I rebelled, the more Mom clamped down. The more she clamped down, the more I rebelled.

Take the night before when we had the blow-up. Okay, so I *was* a few minutes late coming in. Well, maybe it was more like an *hour* late. Anyway, just as I expected, Mom followed me into my room. "Where were you all this time, Shelly? I worry about you when you're late. *Anything* could have happened! Why didn't you call me?" On and on and on.

As usual, Mom threw in a little scripture for good measure, as if she didn't drill me on memory verses at our breakfast table *every morning of the world*! "Remember, Shelly," she'd said that night, "the Bible says, 'Children, obey your parents ... If you honor your father and mother, yours will be a long life, full of blessing" (see Ephesians 6:1a, 2b, TLB). Then, she added, "Shelly, your life just shortened by one day!"

"Mom," I yelled, "will you just leave me alone!" When she finally left, I slammed the door behind her.

Today, she was pretending nothing had happened, trying to make us look like the ideal loving family of her dreams. Meantime, after hanging up the telephone, I was sitting there, thinking, *What is all this horseback-riding business? Mom isn't even a horse person! She just wants to know what I'm doing every minute.*

Half-heartedly, I pulled on my riding boots, then shrugged over to the dresser. Reaching for a comb, my hand brushed against the necklace Mom had given me for my last birthday. *I'd better wear this or she'll ask where it is.* Reluctantly, I fastened the silver chain around my neck and straightened the pendant—the silver outline of a heart with its message, in script, suspended inside: "Sweet Sixteen." *Yeah, sure, Mom.*

By the time I got to the barn, Dad had already saddled our dun/Overo paint, Miss Char-Deck—we usually called her Charcey—and Mom was swinging into the saddle. "Mom, *what* are you doing?" I shrieked. "You've never ridden Charcey before! She's a *big* horse." *I cannot believe this woman! I thought. She'll do anything to be part of my life. And I just want her out of it!*

While Dad was bridling the Arabian named Babe, Mom discovered her stirrups were too long. Before Dad could turn around to adjust them, Charcey charged away at full gallop. *What has gotten into Charcey?*

Scared and inexperienced, Mom probably reacted by doing all the wrong things. Whatever the reason, Charcey was out of control. Never had I seen that horse run so fast, her mane and tail flying in the wind! It was as though she had to show off what a quarter horse is bred to do: win short-distance races. With every stride of her powerful haunches, she gained speed.

I watched, horrified, as Charcey's hooves beat at the earth, faster, and faster—like something possessed, a thousand pounds of straining muscle thundering across the pasture.

With lightning speed, Charcey reached a corner of the pasture fence—a place of decision. Should she jump? *No. Too high with a ditch on the other side.* Other choice? *Make a ninety-degree turn.* Charcey turned. Mom flew high into the air, crashed through a barbed-wire fence, and landed on the sun-parched ground.

THUD!

Then—*nothing.* Except for Charcey's hoof beats as she tore back to the barn.

Dear God! No! No! This can't be happening! I sprinted across the pasture, out-running Dad on the Arabian. "Mom! Mom!" *Please, God, don't let her be dead! I didn't mean it, God. I don't really want her out of my life! Please!*

The barbed wire was holding her in an almost kneeling position. Her right wrist and hand dangled the wrong way, her neck and head were turned as if broken, and blood oozed from gashes on her back. *Is she breathing? Please, God,* she *thinks I don't love her.* "Mom?"

After what seemed an eternity, I heard a moan—then a weak, "I'm okay, Shelly."

"Mom! Oh, Mom! I didn't mean to be so hateful. I *do* love you, Mom." Ever so carefully, I began untangling her hair from the barbed wire, barely able to see through my tears. "Oh, Mama, I'm so sorry. I'm so sorry."

"I know, Shelly," Mom somehow managed, while I made one last tug on her now-shredded pink sweater and freed her from the wire.

"We've got to get you to the hospital," Dad said, jumping back astride Babe and turning her toward the barn. "I'll call an ambulance."

"No," Mom said, and because she was a nurse, we listened. "You can carry me in the van."

It wasn't easy, but we did it. Dad barreled down the highway, all the while trying to raise a police escort on the two-way radio. Meanwhile, I did what Mom had taught me—I quoted scripture, the first one that popped into my head.

"Rejoice in the Lord always," I said, close to her ear, "and again I say rejoice" (Philippians 4:4, KJV). For *once*, I must have done the right thing. Because Mom, through all her pain, started quoting scripture, one verse after another, all the way to the hospital.

Mom spent most of the next three months in a wheelchair, and during that time the two of us did a lot of talking. "Mom," I told her, "I know I act a lot like Charcey did that day of the accident. I just want to charge through life without being held back, not missing anything."

"Yes, Shelly, and I always want to be in control, to make sure things go right. To protect you from getting hurt."

We decided because we were very different, we'd probably *always* clash over one thing or another.

We agreed on something else, too. That we loved each other, no matter what.

Still, I felt a need to do something more to make things right. One day at school I asked permission to speak at our chapel service. Standing on stage behind the microphone, I took a deep breath and started. To the other students, to the faculty, and especially to Mom who sat in the back of the room in her wheelchair, I said, "I want to apologize for all the mistakes I've made this year, mistakes that have hurt others. Worst of all, they have hurt my mom."

I told them how hateful I had been to my mother. How I had yelled at her to stay out of my life. Then I told them about Mom's accident. About how at the thought of losing her, I realized she is my very best friend. That she wanted only what is best for me. "Please, you guys," I begged my fellow students, "tell your mother you love her. Don't wait too late, like I almost did."

I looked back at Mom who was beaming, while dabbing at her eyes with a tissue. "Mom," I said, voice quivering, "I ask you to forgive me. I ask *God* to forgive me."

As if on cue, one of Mom's Bible verses popped into my head. "If we confess our sins, He is faithful and just to forgive us our sins ..." (1 John 1:9a, KJV). *Thank you, God, for believing in me, even when I disappoint you over and over."*

Just like Mom! I realized in a flash of insight. Instinctively, I reached up and caressed the silver pendant at my neck. My fingers traced the intricate lettering, "Sweet Sixteen." *Sixteen? Yes. Sweet? Hardly But I will try, Mom,* I smiled through my tears. *I will try.*

Leaving the platform, suddenly I became aware of a new-for-me feeling. One that said, "It's okay, Shelly, to let your mom into your life.

Even when you're sweet sixteen."

CHAPTER 3

Jesus, Our Anchor

Trusting Him When Seas Stay Stormy

I will not doubt, though all my ships at sea
Come drifting home with broken masts and sails;
I shall believe the Hand which never fails,
From seeming evil worketh good to me;
And, though I weep because those sails are battered,
Still will I cry, while my best hopes lie shattered,
"I trust in Thee."

—Ella Wheeler Wilcox, from "Faith" in
Best Loved Religious Poems

Comes the Dawn

"He stilled the storm to a whisper; the waves of the sea were hushed. They were glad when it grew calm, and He guided them to their desired haven."
Psalm 107:29-30, NIV

A devotional, written for the families of 9/11

In times of fear or terrible loss, we wonder if the sun ever will shine again. That is how I felt when my young husband fought "incurable" cancer.

Frantically grasping for a lifeline, something to hold onto, I discovered the book *Drumbeat of Love* by Lloyd J. Ogilvie. The author addresses the dilemma of when problems don't have quick answers, of when we desperately need an anchor in the storm. In writing about the story found in Acts 27 of the Bible—when the Apostle Paul's ship is caught in a violent storm during the night—Dr. Ogilvie says: "There are times when there is nothing to do but claim the promises and pray for dawn to break.

"Then" he continues, "when morning comes, Christ greets us across the wild and tempestuous sea. 'Peace be still; it is I!'"

So it was that all through our struggle with cancer, I claimed God's promises—and prayed for morning to come. Sure enough, in the midst of our tempest, Jesus came. And calmed my turbulent heart. I pray the same for you.

Dear Lord, comfort those who are hurting. Calm their fears. May they know your grace, your love, your peace—and an early dawn. Amen

Dr. Lloyd J. Ogilvie is an author, a Presbyterian Minister, and has served as chaplain of the United States Senate.

That Night in May

As written for: Marinel Wood

"Lay hold upon the hope set before us: Which hope we have as an anchor of the soul, both sure and steadfast."
Hebrews 6:18b-19a, KJV

For this teenager, a dream date turned into a horrid nightmare.

May 28, 1999—the night my life changed forever. I was a junior in high school, a cheerleader, active in school activities, worlds of friends. Just one more year and I would be heading to the University of Georgia—I pictured myself in my cute red and black outfit, leading cheers in Sanford Stadium.

That night though, having just finished exams, I was planning my best summer ever. I had a date with one of the finest guys ever put on this earth. I had always dreamed of dating Mike, and the chance had come. I mean this guy was a leader in the military school he had graduated the year before. A guy who looked ever so handsome in his uniform. Was I on top of the world that night, or what? I was a free bird, loving life. Until 11:35.

Mike had come back to town to attend some friends' graduation ceremony. We had just left a pre-grad party for those friends when he said, "Let's take a spin."

"Let me drive, Mike," I asked. I thought it best not to remind him he'd had a couple of beers.

"Sure," he said, handing me the keys. We got into his green Acura Integra, his friend Danny crawled onto the back seat.

We'd stopped for a red light, when a white Acura Integra, same model as Mike's, pulled up alongside. The guy stuck his head out the window, "Are you tanked up?"

"Yeah!" Mike yelled back.

They must be talking about the tank of nitrous oxide Mike has installed in his car—to give it extra boost, I thought to myself. *It must be a "guy thing."*

"I'll bet I can take you!" the driver of the other car goaded.

"You're on," Mike shot back. "Marinel," he said, opening the passenger side door, "give me the steering wheel. I'll show that guy what this baby can do."

For the moment, I forgot all about why I was driving in the first place. I knew I was not about to drive a racecar. So while Mike jumped out and ran around the back of the car to take the driver's seat, I scooted around the front, and hopped back into the car as a passenger.

Not one of us fastened a seatbelt.

The traffic light turned green. Motors revved, tires screeched as we blasted off like a rocket. Almost instantly the speedometer raced to 50, 60, 70, 80—80 heart-stopping miles per hour! On a heavily traveled city street! I sent up a fervent plea, *Dear God, help me!*

The two lanes lasted less than a half mile. As we flew around a curve, the lanes merged. We found ourselves almost on top of the other Acura. It had stopped in our lane! I screamed, *Mike! Look out!*

Mike swerved. The car went out of control. It started to "fishtail," throwing us into a violent spin. Any thrill of the race was replaced by sickening terror. *Dear Jesus, help!* Tires squealed, the car groaned, screams filled the night air as the tremendous force catapulted us sideways into three sturdy pine trees—like hitting a concrete wall.

Then—black silence.

Four weeks later, for the first time, I managed to force open my eyes. They didn't focus well. *Where am I? Who are these strange people all in white?* I tried to speak. Only a moan came out. I heard voices but I couldn't understand a word, and drifted back into my coma.

After several days of brief waking periods, I felt Mom smoothing my brow and saying, "You're in a hospital, Marinel. You're doing fine." At that point, I couldn't think clearly enough even to wonder why.

Evidently, though, I had turned a corner. Gradually I learned I had suffered severe brain injuries in the accident. Most nights during those weeks I was in a coma, they feared I'd never live until morning.

The part of my brain that was damaged controlled the motor skills. My left side was paralyzed. I could not even swallow. Food arrived to my stomach through a tube. Someone had to brush my teeth, bathe me, and the most humiliating of all—change diapers.

Weeks later, when I could at least *think* again but still couldn't talk, Mom would hold up a board that had numbers, letters, and short words. With great effort, using my one good hand, I pointed to the ones necessary to communicate on the most basic of levels.

Recovery was slow. And frustrating! Every muscle had to be retrained. One day, I was simply trying to hold a spoon when I spilled food all over me. I cried bitter tears as I recalled my life before the accident. I thought of those intricate jumps I did as a cheerleader all through school. *Now I can't even hold a spoon!*

When I finally found my voice, my speech was so halting I feared no one could ever understand me. One day my cousin Lauren came by on one of her regular visits. She greeted me that day with "What's wrong, Marinel?"

"Nothing," I answered.

"I can tell something's wrong,"

"No, nothing," I insisted.

"Marinel, don't you lie to me."

With that I started bawling. "Lauren, I'm not gonna' have any friends after this. I can't talk, I can't walk!"

Lauren came and sat on the edge of my bed, "Marinel," she said, "look at all these flowers, these cards—all from friends who love you."

I was inconsolable. "It's bad enough I'll never be able to lead cheers at the University of Georgia," I wailed, "but no one is even gonna' *like* me. No one's gonna' want to be my boyfriend. No one's gonna' want to marry me. My whole life is thrown away because I made one stupid mistake. This is not fair!"

She grabbed my hand. "Marinel, you look at me and you listen to me right now!"

I looked at her, tears spilling down my cheeks.

"Marinel, give yourself more time. You'll be back enjoying life like you did before. Look how far you've already come!"

Lauren wiped my face then added, "Marinel, you've got tons of friends who love you. They ask about you all the time and can't wait until you get back. Anytime you feel down, you remember that!"

Lauren had to repeat those words many times. Because following the fifty-two days I was in the hospital of Shepherd Spinal Center in Atlanta, I spent eight long months in their rehab center, undergoing intensive therapy of every kind known to man—physical, cognitive, speech, occupational. It was grueling, zapping every ounce of energy.

Like the torture of trying to learn to walk. One particularly difficult day, my physical therapist Terri, propped me up between the railings, which I didn't even have the strength to grasp, especially with my practically useless left hand. With an attendant in back of me and Terri in front, she said, "Now, Marinel, I want you to walk toward me."

My brain said to my legs, "Move." Nothing. I tried, and tried. Perspiration popped out on my forehead. Still—nothing.

"I cannot do this!" I said, gritting my teeth. "This is not happening, Terri."

"Yes, you can."

"No, I *cannot* walk!"

"Yes, you can.

"No! No!" I practically shouted. "Terri, I know you're getting paid to say 'Yes, you can' but I'm telling you, "I can't do it!"

"Marinel, look at me," she said, a loving firmness in her voice "I'm saying this because I *want* you to walk. And I *know* you can. I will help you *until* you can. Try again, Marinel."

That was to be the first of many punishing, often disappointing, sessions, but Terri's determination never faltered.

Early on, my family and attending physicians had decided I should be given information about the accident, only as I asked specific questions. So it was months before I knew the details.

I learned Mike's injuries were not serious. But he was under house arrest awaiting a court date, faced with multiple charges including: serious injury by a motor vehicle; driving under the influence; reckless driving; racing; no seat belt; failure to maintain lane; possession of alcohol by a minor; and the most serious charge—vehicular homicide.

Vehicular homicide because, saddest of all, at impact Danny was thrown through the sunroof of the Acura. He died instantly.

Once home, I talked with Mike on the phone. "I don't blame you for what happened," I told him. "I gave you the keys. We both did something stupid." I meant it, too. I never blamed Mike. Still, I couldn't understand why this had happened to me. Lots of people make stupid decisions and never suffer any consequences. Why did *my* life have to be ruined?

I dreaded going back to school in a wheelchair. How would my friends react? I needn't have worried. At the first basketball game—in the gym where I had led many a cheer—friends sat all around me as we rooted for our Lakeview Lions who were battling it out on the court.

After the game, a bunch of the players called out, "Let's go get dinner!" And away we went! Just like we used to do. *Lauren was right,* I thought, *I can still have fun with my friends.*

Then came the next hurdle, learning to walk. Before basketball season ended, I managed—with much effort and pain, to do just that! Wobbly, but walking! Only then did I learn the doctors had told my parents I probably would never walk again. *Thanks, Terri, for never giving up on me.*

Now, one year after the accident, it's May again. A beautiful spring day and I've got butterflies in my stomach. My school, along with those all over the country, is holding its Prom Promise Assembly. Its purpose is to encourage young people not to go wild with partying—drinking and driving—on prom night. Guess who they invited to give the talk?

What if the people can't understand me? What if I drop the pages of my speech? I fret inwardly, knowing full well that my speech is not back to normal and my hand still shakes. *At least you can walk, Marinel,* I tell myself using my old pep-rally talent, *even though you do have to study each step before you take it.*

Somehow I manage to get onto the stage and to the microphone. *But what's this?* From the time I stand to my feet, the entire audience stands to theirs. Thunderous applause fills the building! *I can't believe it!* I look out into the faces of family, faculty and friends. Throughout my long ordeal, these people have visited me, written me, prayed for me. Their expressions tell me they are here for me once again.

As I muster the courage to speak, I can almost hear Terri saying, "You can do it, Marinel."

Haltingly, I begin, "Come with me as I travel back to this time last year. Let me tell you how my life changed in a matter of twenty seconds, changed because I did something really stupid. I didn't take time to think."

I glance around the auditorium. The students are taking in every word. And Mom isn't the only one dabbing her eyes with a tissue.

Pausing a moment, I send up a quick prayer, *Thank you, God, for bringing me this far. Help me make a difference in these lives.*

My presentation over, I walk back to my seat hearing, "Good for you, Marinel." "Super job!" "You look great!" *These people love me just for being me,* I realize, *even if I never lead another cheer.*

I feel really good, confident. For although I have a long way to go until complete recovery, I know my friends will stick by me. And so will God.

The program over, I step out into a beautiful spring day—a day filled with promise..

⚓

Long Journey Home

As written for: Ruby Bennett

"Yea, I have loved thee with an everlasting love."
Jeremiah 31:3b,KJV

**Now, at last, she had a father. A family.
A heritage. It had been a long journey home.**

I was not quite five that hot August afternoon. At our white frame house in the Mississippi countryside, my little brother and I played on the back porch while Mother and my fifteen-year-old sister, Fanny, ironed clothes in the kitchen.

All had been peace and quiet until, without warning, everything changed. My father had died the year before and Mother hired a man to help with the farm. Now that man, reeking of alcohol, stomped up the back steps and into the kitchen. Soon loud, angry words erupted followed by a frightful "POW!" Mother screamed, "Run, Fanny! Run!" Fanny tore across the porch and down the steps, the man right behind her, pointing a gun.

Then my beautiful mother stumbled out onto the porch. Clutching her chest, blood staining her print dress, she crumpled at my feet. And died.

Out in the cotton field, the man shot Fanny. A neighbor found her—face down in the dirt—badly hurt, but alive.

A few minutes later, my oldest brothers—eleven and fourteen—who had been fishing in the creek, came screaming toward the house, faces mirroring terror. "He ran into the woods. Said he'd kill every last one of us!"

He never came back. But he had made us orphans. Eight orphans nobody wanted.

Before my father married Mother, he had had two families— both wives had died. With the three wives he had twenty-one children. But now, for whatever reason, none of the older stepsiblings offered help. Instead, people came to get us from the Mississippi Children's Home.

They only took five. The other three—11, 14, and 15—were "too old." I didn't know what was happening, but I sensed we'd never again live together as a family.

When they herded us aboard a train, I felt the whole world had abandoned me. Mother had taught that Jesus loves me. But to my young mind, *He* had deserted me, too. I hugged my cloth doll as tight as I could, and stared out the train window as home disappeared forever.

After six months at the Children's Home, the ladies came in one morning to help me dress. "We're taking you to a family for 'approval,'" they said. Soon we set out for Sunflower, Mississippi.

Mr. and Mrs. Norris had asked for a two-year-old girl, with blue eyes and blond curly hair. The only thing I had going for me were the blue eyes. I was too old, had corn-shuck hair, and after running into a swing a few days earlier, had black and blue bruises all over my face. Not exactly the cute little child they had ordered.

Mrs. Norris looked me over. Obviously disappointed, she told the deliverers, "Go ahead and leave her so my husband can see her. But be sure to come back on Friday to pick her up."

I wasn't eager to stay anyway—they lived in a tent! I'd already told the ladies that brought me, "I don't want to live in a rag house." They explained the Norrises were "camping out" while building their house and would soon be moving.

As it happened, there were *two* tents. One was for cooking. Mr. Norris was a road contractor and Mrs. Norris and her helper cooked for the hired men when they came in from work.

One night, to keep me occupied while she cooked, Mrs. Norris put a board across the arms of a wooden chair, making a sort of desk. As I was busy scribbling along, I looked up and said, "Can I call you Mama? I don't have a mama."

When Mr. Norris came home on Thursday night, he agreed to keep me for a trial period. Next day, when the ladies from the Home came back to get me, Mama said, "She'll be staying."

Finally, I had a daddy. And before long, we moved into the new house. I felt like it was built especially for me. I had my own bedroom, a big yard, and friends to play with. Mr. and Mrs. Norris were wonderful parents. Daddy called me "Pumpkin." He even bought a piano for me to learn to play hymns.

I didn't get to keep my new Daddy long. He came down with pneumonia and died within a week. "Lord, how could you do this to me?" I cried. "I'm just nine years old and already I've lost a mother and two daddies."

As I got older, I worried about the fate of my sisters and brothers. I learned the four younger children eventually were adopted, all in different homes.

But Fanny, only fifteen at the time of the tragedy, spent several months in the hospital. Then she, like the boys, 11 and 14, was farmed out to whoever would take her for a little while. All three were made to work like adults with no opportunity for schooling.

I resented my stepbrothers and stepsisters for not rescuing us when we needed them. To let us be scattered to the winds.

It was as if we didn't even belong to the same family. Just one more reason to wonder why God had forgotten all about me.

I was thirteen when I learned that God knew exactly where I was. Mama had asked me to clean the library shelves in the living room. I loved those shelves—they reached all the way to the ceiling. Moving and dusting books, I picked up an old Bible of hers, one she had replaced years ago. A yellowed newspaper clipping fell out. The headlines startled me. "Mother slain, leaves eight children." It was about *us!* I sat down on the couch to read, reliving the horror.

"Mama," I said, handing her the clipping as she came into the room, "Did you know this is about my Mother?"

She scanned the headline. "No, Ruby," she said softly, sitting down beside me, "I recall clipping the article but don't know why I saved it. I had no idea it was about your Mother."

At that moment, if God had spoken audibly to me, it could not have been clearer. His message? "I've never forsaken you, Ruby. I was with you when they carried you to the Children's Home; I gave you the words when you asked Mrs. Norris if she would be your mama; I put love for you in the hearts of Mr. and Mrs. Norris; and I had her save that article so you would find it at this important age." Oh, how I needed that reassurance. *God loves me!*

Now it is fifty years later and my husband had just come home from a business trip. "Ruby, did you know your name is on a marker out by the highway?"

"Whatever are you talking about, Taylor?"

"Over in Summit," he explained. "Your name, along with those of all your father's children, is on a huge marble marker!"

"I've got to see that," I said, shocked beyond words. At first opportunity we drove one hundred ninety miles to take a look.

Sure enough, at the entrance to the old family property, there stood a new marble marker, measuring all of 6 x 8 ft. The inscription at top: "BOLIAN FARM" Below it reads, "In memory of William Bolian, father of the following children." Just underneath are three columns—one for each wife—and underneath, in chronological order, the names of all twenty-one children. Third from the last is Ruby. That's *me!*

How very unusual, I thought, thoroughly embarrassed.

"At least," I told Taylor, "the older ones finally acknowledge that Mother's children are members of the family. I now have something permanent to attest that I have roots." I was beginning to like that marker, after all.

I read again the scripture chiseled into stone at the bottom of the marker: "For God so loved the world, that He gave His only begotten Son, that whosoever believeth in Him should not perish but have everlasting life" (John 3:16, KJV).

From my far distant past a hazy picture formed: *I'm a small child, snuggled in my Daddy's lap. He is reading to the family from the Bible. What love I feel. How warm, how secure.* Standing there, observing that marker, I felt close to my father—as if, for the first time, I *knew* him.

As Taylor and I drove home, I thanked God for showing me that early in my life, Daddy had instilled in me his faith. *Lord,* I prayed, *thank you for reminding me in this unique way that my father loved his little girl.*

Whereupon God dropped into my mind another Bible verse. "This is my commandment, that ye love one another, as I have loved you" (John 15:12, KJV).

That means I must forgive my siblings who let me down, I told myself to the hum of the car's engine. Suddenly it occurred to me that the Lord's commandment to love was for my sake as well as for others. I had carried around the burden of bitterness much too long. *Besides,* I told myself, *they have given me back my father.*

By the time Taylor turned the car into our driveway, my heart already felt lighter—lighter and at peace with the world. It had been a long journey home.

God, Are You Out There?

"So do not fear, for I am with you."
Isaiah 41:10a, NIV

A Devotional

One night my friend Carolyn, accompanied by her three-year-old daughter Julie, walked down the street to visit a neighbor. It turned out to be a pitch-black night without a moon in sight.

The two found themselves on an unlighted driveway, long and winding. The silhouettes of bare tree limbs, whipped by the wind, looked to Julie like huge monster arms, just waiting to snatch her. Suddenly, in the nearby underbrush, leaves rustled. Julie, holding onto her Mother's hand, tightened her grip, stopped dead in her tracks, snuggled just as close as she could get, cocked her head to one side the better to listen, and in all seriousness called out, "God, are you out there?"

I chuckle each time I think about that scene. But haven't we all been there? Who among us has not in our heart cried out, "God, are you out there?" During the long nights while we waited outside a hospital Intensive Care Unit; or when we were out of work and the bills piled up; or those times of extreme loneliness when we felt as if no one cared. How reassuring then to claim His promise, "I am with you."

I recall another story of God's protective care. It seems that one night in Africa, missionary and explorer David Livingstone, his life threatened by natives, said, "I read again that Jesus said, "Lo, I am with you always" (Matthew 28:20, KJV). It's the word of a gentleman and that's the end of it. I will not cross the river by night furtively as I had intended."

So it is that we, too, can face the future with courage, knowing Jesus will be with us. After all, it's the word of a gentleman and that's the end of it.

Thank you, Jesus, for the many times your reassuring Presence has calmed my own fears.

ValuJet Flight 592

As written for: Martha Carter

"The best prayers have often more groan than words."
John Bunyan

They had flown down together for the cruise. But now—the unthinkable ...

Sunday, May 12, 1996. A pall permeated the Miami terminal, teeming now with people, most talking in hushed tones. I sat stone-faced, lost in my own private nightmare. I was jolted awake to hear, "ValuJet Flight 592 to Atlanta now boarding." I gathered my bags, then drew back. *A week ago, we flew down together. How can I go home without them?*

Just yesterday morning, after a marvelous Caribbean cruise, the seven of us—retirees all—stood on deck of the magnificent *Sovereign of the Sea*, hating for the week to be over. The ship's whistle signaled we were coming into port; Pier 5 bustled with the activity of shore hands; and the public address system sprang to life: "Those catching flights out will disembark first."

There followed much giggling, and gathering of packages containing souvenirs for children and grandchildren—

97

wonderful little hand-carved statues, colorful baskets, native art work—each carefully chosen for the special recipient.

We all spoke at once to our departing foursome, "It's been great!" "See you back in Gainesville." "We'll get together next week and enjoy the pictures." We clutched at our new tropical hats as we hugged and said goodbye to those of our group catching ValuJet Flight 592.

In a short while, the rest of us—Bill Hackett, Mary Tyner, and I—left the ship, drove into Miami to enjoy a quick lunch with relatives, and soon after one o'clock began our tour of the city.

Suddenly, great hordes of siren-blaring, emergency vehicles careened past us. "What in the world?" I exclaimed. I'd never seen anything like it. Upon learning a jetliner had plummeted into the Everglades, a knot formed in the pit of my stomach. "Don't worry," someone said, "*their* plane was due to leave around noon." Still, in my heart I knew it was theirs. Too soon, my fears were confirmed. Saturday's ValuJet Flight 592 had nose-dived and buried itself in that vast swamp. With hardly a trace. I was inconsolable.

Now I would never see them again—my dear friends Louise Stanley and her husband, Hugh; my very close friend Ruth Wolfe; and Ruth's lifetime good friend from South Carolina, Elizabeth Gabriel. It was too much to accept.

"How will I ever face their children?" I asked myself. "Tomorrow is Mother's Day and they were going to be together." *Lord, help me to know how to help them.*

A mutual friend from home phoned. Betty was distraught. She reported that Ruth's son Judson had learned the news from the airline. But Louise's daughters still didn't know. "Martha," Betty managed through her tears, "You've got to call Lynn and Julie. I can't do it."

It was the hardest thing I ever did. I wanted to assure them their parents' final week was one of much joy. But I was too grief-stricken myself to talk much about it. Maybe later I could show them our snapshot collection and share all the fun things we did. *Oh, no! I can't,* I realized with a stab of fresh pain; *Ruth was the one always taking pictures. And the rolls of undeveloped film were with her!*

My son phoned from Georgia. "I'll drive down to get you, Mom."

"No, Tom," I said, "I appreciate the offer. But if I don't fly now, I'll never fly again."

It took every ounce of courage I could muster to board Sunday's ValuJet Flight 592. I couldn't help thinking: *If we three had not decided to stay an extra day....*

Soon after takeoff, the flight path took us over the Everglades and the crash scene. Aboard our plane there was a reverence, the only sounds those of the plane's engines and my sobbing. I thought of those 110 persons who died in one second, including my four friends and the pilot who had brought us all to Miami. Each of them had unfinished plans. Each of them had family and friends who loved them.

On the remainder of the trip home, conflicting emotions fought for dominance in my tortured mind. Unable to forget for a moment the horrible tragedy, I tried to recall our wonderful week aboard the luxurious cruise ship—leisurely lolling on deck in the sun, enjoying marvelous meals, playing late-night bingo with no schedules to worry about—we laughed a lot, always and about everything, we laughed.

A kaleidoscope of scenes skipped around in my consciousness—shore excursions at the ports of call where we traded snorkeling adventures for great shopping opportunities. And for watching native craftsmen demonstrate woodturning, pottery making, basket weaving....

I recalled the afternoon Louise and I opted for some time in the hot tub out on ship's deck. Suddenly it began to rain and Louise donned her huge straw hat to protect her hairdo. We sat there and giggled like two young teenagers.

Or the day we all were lounging on deck chairs, chatting about one thing or another. The six of us from Gainesville started recalling our long friendships, attending church together, playing bridge every week, going on tours, keeping up with the lives of each other's children and grandchildren.

Elizabeth—the out-of-towner—added, "Ruth and I have been friends all our lives. We went to school together, to college together, dated together and were in each other's wedding. We've helped with each other's children. And I guess we'll die together."

I shivered at the truth of it.

Upon returning home, I found my entire city in shock and mourning. I was of little use in ministering to their many friends, let alone to their children. The fact that bodies were never recovered made acceptance of the deaths even more difficult. Searchers found few identifiable items in the murky swamp.

Weeks later, Ruth's son phoned. "Martha, you're not going to believe this! They've found Mom's handbag!" In the salt-water soaked pocketbook was her camera, loaded with exposed film. With little hope, Judson left the rolls with a developer, explaining the importance of the film. To everyone's amazement, most of the pictures are viewable—hazy and watermarked, but viewable. Judson immediately mailed sets to each family.

I felt I was handling something almost holy as I carefully looked through my set of the prints. Now I had something tangible to show the children. Now I could tell them about all the fun, wacky things we did on the cruise. I could assure them that their parents enjoyed to the fullest their last week on earth.

Thank you, Lord, for this answer to prayer.

Prints in hand, I phoned Judson in South Carolina. "You know how your Mom hugged everybody she met and took a snapshot? " I began. He knew exactly what I meant. Ruth loved life and everybody in it.

"Well," I went on, "see those adorable little children in hats ...? Oh, and this one," I said, looking at another print. "There we are having dinner on ship—all seven of us, having a wonderful time. Your mother, Judson, made *everything* fun." On the other end of the phone line, I could sense a slow smile.

Next I would phone Lynn and Julie. *They will love the story of their mom and me in the hot tub.*

Sharing memories. Precious memories of treasured friendships.

Friendships I shall treasure always.

The Girl Who Lost Her Smile

As written for: Kim Davis

In time of trouble
It is comforting to know
God is still on his throne
And He loves me.
—gcs
"The Thought"

A teenager learns the value of inner beauty.

When I was 16, I lost my smile. I remember the morning it happened. I'd given my makeup one last check, grabbed my softball uniform, and dashed out the door. "'Bye, Annabell," I'd called out to our pet dachshund. "I'll see you tonight after the game."

I never made it to the game.

On our way there, the car I was in hit a truck. Instead of going to Greensboro to play with the Walton Academy Bulldogs against the Nathanael Green Patriots, I was rushed by ambulance to St. Mary's Hospital in Athens. My skull had been fractured, and the doctors feared I might not live through the night.

Two days later, I opened my eyes. *Where am I?* I asked myself. *Why is there an IV needle in my arm? And my family— why are they crying? What is wrong with these people?*

Only after several days had passed did Mom say, "Kim, there's something I have to tell you. The blow to your head injured the nerve controlling the left side of your face. For now, honey, it's paralyzed."

"Hey," I thought, "it can't be that bad."

But it was. When they finally allowed me to look in a mirror, the face I saw looked like that of a rag doll—a rag doll with the stitching on one side pulled way too tight.

I stared into the mirror and tried to smile. I couldn't.

"It's OK," I said, trying to make my mother feel better. "It won't last long." In my heart, you see, I just knew God would make it right. Hadn't I publicly dedicated my life to Him just two days before this happened? Besides, my junior-senior prom was coming up in two weeks. I *had* to be ready for that.

The next week a specialist came in. "Kim," he said, "I'm afraid this paralysis is permanent. If there's no regeneration within a month, we'll have to operate and see how much we can reconstruct."

After he left, I almost drowned in my tears. "What am I going to do?" I asked of the empty room. "Nobody will want to look at this ugly face. Nobody will ever ask me out again." I buried my face in my pillow. "How can God let this happen to me? I can't even smile!"

The day I was to go home from the hospital, Mom packed my things. "Kim," she said, "I'm certain your spirits will improve when you get home."

"I guess so," I sighed, "but I dread it. What will my friends say when they see me?"

"If you forget about your face," Mom replied, "probably everyone else will, too. Remember, Kim, a smile begins on the *inside*."

When we pulled into the driveway, I tried to whistle for Annabell. I couldn't even pucker my lips. Eventually, I gave up and called to her. "Here, Annabell. Here, girl."

Annabell hung back, her ears and tail drooping, her eyes questioning. *I don't believe this,* I thought. *My own dog can't accept me.*

She wasn't the only one. Oh, there were hugs and kisses enough when I went back to school, but I saw pity in the eyes of my friends, and I hated it. I wanted to tell them, "Hey, it's me, Kim! I'm the same person I was before the accident. Can't you treat me the same? Can't you accept me the way I am?"

Yet maybe *I* was the one who couldn't accept me. How could I? I couldn't even smile.

My facial nerve didn't regenerate on its own, so Mom and Dad flew with me to Pittsburgh for surgery. "Kim, recovery of movement will take time," the surgeon reported afterwards, "but your face will never be 100 percent like it was before. I'm sorry."

So was I. Back in Georgia, weeks passed with no signs of progress. I still couldn't move even the tiniest muscle on the left side of my face. All I could do was sulk—sulk, and stretch out on the green lounge chair in our backyard, with Annabell lying underneath.

"Why did you let this happen to me?" I would ask God. "My life is ruined and you don't even care! And if *you* don't love me, who does? Nobody, that's who."

Gradually, however, my broken relationship with God began to bother me even more than did my frozen face. As a result, I began reading books about other young people—people who'd triumphed over tragedy. I was looking for answers. I needed answers. I even took my Bible out into the yard with me, to look for even the smallest hint of Providence.

One morning after a rain, I was again out back in my favorite chair. The wet earth smelled good, and I reached out to give

Annabell a little love pat. "Good old Annabell," I told her. "*You* love me, no matter how I look."

I don't know how to explain it, but somehow Annabell's love touched me, melting my bitterness and washing it away. With that gone, my heart felt as fresh and clean as the rain-swept earth. Then it was that God planted a thought in me. "Kim," God said. "I love you too. I've never deserted you. I've been with you all along."

Had I been so wrapped up in self-pity that I'd not let God comfort me? That must have been so, for now His presence changed my whole way of thinking.

I recalled a verse that had meant so much to another accident victim—one I'd just read about. "We know that all things work together for good," it said in Romans 8:28, "to them that love God."

"*All* things work together ..." the verse said. Could that possibly hold true for me as well? I wanted to believe that it could. I wanted to believe that good could come out of my horrible experience. I wanted this to be true, and that's why I determined then and there that I would do my part toward recovering my smile, then trust God to do His.

Mustering up all my courage, I took a part-time job at a fast-food restaurant. It wasn't easy for me to face the public, but I hung in there.

One day a small customer asked me, "Why do you smile crooked?"

"Because I'm special," I told him. It was a true enough answer, I suppose, even if it couldn't make my problems disappear.

My next hurdle was deciding to go out for cheerleading. Would my friends elect me again? Would they vote for me—a cheerleader who couldn't even smile? They would, and they did!

It was soon after this, on a Tuesday night in August, that I knelt in church and confessed to God that I'd been angry with

Him. "Please forgive me, Lord," I prayed. "This time I truly surrender everything to you—my plans, my dreams, and even my face."

A short time later, our family was returning from a short vacation in Florida. Dad drove the van, while I sat in the front seat doing the facial exercises my doctor had prescribed. That's when it happened.

"My mouth moved," I squealed. I fished a mirror from my bag to get a closer look. "It did! Look, I can move it! Just a little bit, but I *can* move it!" Laughing and crying, we pulled off the interstate so that we could pull ourselves together. It was a glorious day!

That was several years ago. Now it is a clear, cool night in May, and I am on stage with the other graduating seniors of the Brenau-Hall School of Nursing in Gainesville, Georgia. Sitting there with my friends, all of us stiff and starched in our white uniforms and tiny caps, my mind wanders back to the day when I lost my smile.

I recall the surgeon's words. "Kim," he'd said. "Your face will never be 100 percent like it was before."

He was right.

Since then I've learned, though, that the very best smiles really are those on the inside—those that show themselves in service to others. Those are the smiles that mean the most, and those are the smiles that anyone can share.

On the Brenau College stage, I hear the words, "Kimberly Delynne Davis." I step forward to receive my nursing pin. I walk down the stairs into the auditorium where my parents present me with a long-stemmed rose. I kiss them both. "Thank You, Lord," I silently pray, "for *everything.*"

Then, I smile.

And I think God does too.

When Trouble Comes

Though your world is crumbling
And darkness threatens to overwhelm,
Don't despair. Look up.
See? There's a small break in the clouds.
A shaft of light beams down
Changing everything.
Yes, I know, the world around you
Is still dark.
But, now, you know
That someday
Light will come
And that is enough
For now.

— Gloria Cassity Stargel

Written while praying—and waiting—for Joe's healing from cancer.

When God Speaks in Whispers

Darkest clouds will have a rainbow,
Light upon your path will glow,
God is faithful who has promised,
I have always found it so.
—Birdie Bell*

God comforts a grieving family
in a very special way.

"Hurry, Margaret," I called out to my sister after checking the skies through Mother's kitchen window. "Those storm clouds are getting darker." Low temperatures were setting records in north Georgia and the weatherman was giving dire predictions.

Numb with grief, the two of us bundled up against the sub-zero wind, climbed into her little red Volkswagen, and drove toward Alta Vista Cemetery. Our mother had been laid to rest that afternoon and we wanted to see her grave after the arrangements of pink flowers—Mother's favorites—had been placed on top.

"I still can't believe the funeral director refused to put up a tent," Margaret said. "*Everybody always* has a tent."

"I can't believe it either," I told her. "I was distraught when he told me his intentions. But he insisted the expected blizzard would tear a tent to shreds."

Just then, big fluffs of snow, delicate as angel wings, drifted down from the heavens. A short time later, we stood beside the fresh mound of earth, covered now with pink blossoms. At the head stood a large white floral cross with a life-sized replica of a white dove, poised for flight. And over the whole area, God had spread a protective blanket of white—just enough to cover the newly exposed red clay. But not so much that the pink blooms could not peek through.

It was quite a beautiful scene when it could have been so terrible. We felt comforted. As if God had wrapped *us* in a protective blanket of His *love*, reassuring us that He was taking care of Mother—and of us.

How like a loving Father, speaking to us in such a gentle whisper. And to think: we would have missed this special blessing if we'd had our way about putting the tent in place. It seems that sometimes *not* getting our way is the best way of all.

As we slowly drove away, we stole one last glance at the peaceful scene. It is etched on our hearts—forever.

* From her poem "I Have Always Found It So"
Best-Loved Religious Poems

Death of a Village

God is our refuge and strength, a very present help
in trouble. Therefore will not we fear, though the earth
be removed, and though the mountains be carried
into the midst of the sea.
Psalm 46:1-2, KJV

A Hawaiian vacation turns into something more.

It is an unsettling experience for a volcano to wipe out an entire village just when you're visiting that island. That's what happened during my first trip to Hawaii.

I long had dreamed of visiting our 50th State. So when my son Randy invited me to go along on a trip, I accepted with enthusiasm.

Soon after arrival on the Big Island, I learned that one doesn't just *visit* Hawaii. One *becomes* Hawaii. The spirit of the Islands gets into your blood. Its wonderfully pleasant trade winds, its incredibly beautiful iridescent ocean, the warm hospitality of its people, the glimpses of an ancient culture—all transport you into a totally different world.

In our vacation condo by the sea, I quickly unpacked, donned my new flowered muumuu that reached to the sand,

and draped a lei of plumeria blossoms around my neck. I was ready to *become* Hawaii.

So it was with some concern that I heard Randy's news when he returned from a walk. "Did I tell you one of the volcanoes here is still active?"

"No," I said, holding in mid-air the pitcher of pineapple juice I had been pouring. Glancing at his face to see if he might be kidding, I added, "I don't recall your mentioning that."

"I understand it's always been considered a relatively safe volcano," he said, "but now it's threatening a village." He had my full attention with *that* news and my heart went out to those people, my new friends. *How frightful that must be for them.*

There in our tropical paradise, it was difficult to imagine that just thirty miles away a volcano was spewing molten lava. However, my sensitive respiratory system soon became aware of sulfurous fumes in the air. And from the tables out on the lanai, I wiped away a film of gray volcanic dust.

With the black lava fields all around and now an active volcano, one remembers anew how these islands were formed. How over millions of years, volcanic eruptions that began on the ocean floor kept building up hard surfaces until they finally appeared above water. The result is this intriguing land of contrasts—volcanic deserts and ocean-swept coastlines, rolling pasturelands, lush tropical valleys and snow-capped mountains—all within Hawaii's 93 by 76 miles.

That week in early May of 1990, the flow from the Puu O'o vent of Kilauea Crater picked up speed. The volcano became front-page headlines and television newscasts aimed their cameras toward the village of Kalapana. Residents there had watched the progress of the creeping mass coming toward them since the eruption began January 3, 1983.

For after that spectacular "fountaining" of the volcano—that explosion from deep within the earth, which shoots fire a thousand feet into the air—the liquid rock continued to ooze out of the vent in a hot, gray mass. Looking like something

111

from a horror movie, it spread out, going its own way. At 2,000 degrees, it consumed everything in its path.

On its way to the sea, the flow filled low places—burning vegetation, boiling away ponds, and cutting down utility poles and tall trees. Yet the people of the village kept hoping against hope that the fiery assault somehow would miss them.

It had been an agonizingly slow death for Kalapana. Now the end came quickly as the lava flowed faster—and faster. What had been an orderly evacuation gave way to panic that day, as residents grabbed whatever they could and fled, just minutes before the hot lava covered the village's only remaining road, leaving Kalapana encircled by the relentless flow that devoured—burned or buried—142 dwellings.

"If only there were something we could do to help," I sighed. "Yet the last thing they need right now is a lot of tourists getting in the way." *There is something I can do, though*, I told myself. *I can pray for those people undergoing such trauma. I can pray they will know God's peace in the midst of the storm.*

"Have you seen this?" Randy asked the next day, handing me a newspaper. It showed a particularly touching picture of a little church building, loaded on a trailer, being moved away from the path of destruction. It barely made it out before the onrushing lava overtook the escape route.

I read that the name of the historic little Catholic Church is Star of the Sea. However, it is known as "The Painted Church" because of the brilliant religious folk art which graces the ceiling and walls. The simple white structure with its colorful interior is featured in the Hawaiian points-of-interest books.

As for the displaced persons of Kalapana, many were living in tents set up at the nearby Harry K. Brown Park along the beach. Soon, this area, too, was being invaded by the fiery fingers of lava—smoke, steam and acid fumes creating a health hazard. When the road caught fire, the burning asphalt generated thick black clouds and additional noxious fumes.

Now, the lava was striking salt water, causing much roaring, hissing, and crackling, and producing hydrochloric acid and other potentially hazardous emissions in the blast of steam. The officials cautioned of respiratory problems for those who lingered too long.

I grieved for the people of Kalapana. Some of them had lived there for generations. They gathered in the park now to say good-bye to their homes, their dreams, their way of life. They sought out old friends, embracing warmly, smiling —more than a few of them smiling through tears.

In the midst of their own grief, though, the people knew that here is where creation and destruction meet. This is the way their homeland was formed, and is the way it continues to grow. They knew that, even now, the volcano is breathing new life and adding new land for generations yet to come.

Witnessing this phenomenon made me ponder the awesome power of this One, of whom it is said in His Word: "May the glory of the Lord endure forever; may the Lord rejoice in His works, Who looks on this earth and it quakes and trembles; Who touches the mountains and they smoke!" (Psalm 104:31-32, AMP).

Most native Hawaiians are Christians and not far away, by the side of the road, the Star of the Sea church swayed in the wind as it sat atop its trailer—a silent symbol of devotion to the Lord God.

I returned home to the mainland with a prayer for the people of Kalapana. I prayed they would gain strength and hope from the rescue of that brave little church. And that wherever the church put down new roots, the people, too, could replant and rebuild. Rebuild a community of faith. Faith in this One, our Most High God, Sovereign of the Universe.

NOTE: Kalapana became the second American community to be destroyed by a volcanic eruption, the first being Kapoho in 1960. Earlier, before Hawaii became a state, an eruption in 1926 sent lava over the little fishing village of Hoopuloa. (Information about earlier village destructions from Honolulu's *The Sunday Star-Bulletin & Advertiser*, May 6, 1990, Page A9)

For Such a Time As This

"I thank my God upon every remembrance of you."
Philippians 1:3, KJV

The author says goodbye to Misty Dawn.

She came to us with fear and trembling. She left with our hearts. Her name was Misty Dawn.

But wait, I'm getting ahead of my story.

It was on a blustery, winter's night that I answered the doorbell's ring to find young Joey Lancaster and his Mom. Joey was holding a huge bundle of long silver fur. From that bundle of fur shone two great-big yellow-green eyes on an adorable, pug-nosed face. And draped under Joey's arm was a long, silver plume-like tail. "That's the prettiest cat I ever saw," I said as I ushered them in from the cold.

This was to be a get-acquainted meeting—Joey had proven allergic to cats and they needed to find a home for nine-month-old Misty. Being a cat person, myself, I agreed to their letting her stay the weekend—"on trial." I had no way of knowing that we would need her even more than she needed us.

Misty wasn't sure she wanted *us* either and obviously was *not* happy among strangers in a new environment. She crouched behind furniture or stalked the perimeters of the house, seeking escape.

Next day was no better. I phoned the veterinarian for advice. "I wouldn't adopt a full-grown cat," he said. "They don't easily transfer their affection." And truth be told, I really wanted a little kitten. On top of that, both our sons, though away at college, urged me to wait for a kitten.

I phoned Joey, "I'm afraid it's not going to work," I said.

He sounded disappointed. "Would you mind just keeping her a few more days until I can find her a home?" he asked.

"Sure, I can do that."

A week later, Randy called from school, "Mother, do you still have Misty?"

"Yes."

"Well, I've been thinking," he said, "maybe we ought to keep her."

"I've been thinking the same thing," I responded.

Rick whole-heartedly agreed and before long, with lots of tender, loving care, Misty knew she had found a home. She proved to be the most gentle of creatures with the sweetest of personalities.

Within days, however, it became evident the time had come for her to be spayed. The afternoon Joe and I picked her up at the veterinarian's office following her surgery, we had just left *our* physician's office where we learned that Joe, himself, required immediate surgery. The three of us were about to embark on a journey none of us wanted to take.

Thus began a four-year battle against a virulent strain of cancer—a fierce battle for Joe's life. We were swept along in a raging river, its waters wiping out all solid ground. During those first days and weeks, Misty was the one I turned to for solace. She was there when I cried bitter tears. And when I prayed fervent prayers. All during the year of debilitating treatments, Misty quietly and patiently provided a loving presence. When Joe became depressed and pulled away from close emotional contact, Misty's relaxed purr while she curled up in my lap provided comfort.

The following year, as a result of my praying and Joe's urging, I found myself back in college, a first-quarter sophomore after an absence of 27 years! I recall how difficult was that first quarter. Just trying to read next day's psychology lesson put me to sleep. It was Misty who kept me company while I studied late into the night.

By the time I received that degree from Brenau, I believed God was healing Joe. And further, I believed He wanted me to write about our experience. So Misty and I began work on my book, "The Healing, One Family's Victorious Struggle With Cancer." It took four years; four years with Misty curled up in the top out-basket on the corner of my desk.

All was not work, however. Being very photogenic, Misty appeared in some rather interesting publications. Modern Romance, for instance! In our living room sits a life-size white ceramic cat. Misty evidently felt some kinship and often visited with it. I managed to get a photo of them side-by-side in the same exact pose, standing regally with tails wrapped gracefully around front paws. You can hardly tell which is the live cat. The magazine featured that picture of Misty in their Pet Column.

Another photo op came one night during a presidential debate. I was relaxing in the green recliner, Misty curled up behind my head. As the hour grew late and the debate grew boring, I stood up to go to bed. By now Misty was in a deep sleep, spread-eagled on top of the headrest. A picture of her in that *caring for nothing* position appeared in our local newspaper under the title, "Debate? What Debate?"

Misty took part in our family celebrations too: best of all, Joe was set free from cancer. Rick married and we gained a lovely daughter-in-law. Then Tyndale House published our book. And there, on the back cover, is Misty—right in the forefront of our family photo.

For nineteen precious years, Misty was family. Nineteen years of our daily brushing sessions while we "talked it over." Nineteen years of trials—of triumphs.

But, as time will do, it took its toll. One night, while Misty and I sat on the couch watching television, suddenly she rolled off onto the floor, shaking violently. Her eyes mirrored terror—as did my own. I fell to my knees and tried to calm her little body. "God, "I cried out, "please help Misty!" Slowly, the seizure subsided leaving both of us weak—and frightened.

It proved to be the first of several such episodes. And each time, I cried and prayed. And each time she grew weaker. I think she hung on because she didn't want to leave me and I guess I was selfish. I just couldn't give her up.

Then arthritis took over and robbed her of her dignity. Finally, when I saw every moment was painful for her—how she could no longer even groom herself when she had always been so fastidious—I knew the time had come. I would have to let her go.

Her doctor of all those years offered to come to our house rather than putting her through the trauma of going to his office. All that afternoon, I sat and held her. I thought back to all Misty and our family had been through together, especially facing Joe's illness. *Surely God sent you to us for such a time as this.* I told her how much I loved her, how beautiful she was, and what a fine family member she made. "I'll never forget you, Misty."

When the kind doctor left, Joe brought in the little wooden coffin a friend had made. He had even etched her name on top. We placed Misty there now on the pillow I had covered in gold satin, tucked her blanket around her, and put in two of her favorite toys. I could go no further. While Joe conducted the burial in the woods behind our house, I sat down at the kitchen table and with tears flowing wrote this tribute:

Misty Dawn—Silver-tipped Persian
1972 – 1991 Pet, Companion, Friend
She asked for little.
She gave her all.
The Stargels

CHAPTER 4

Jesus, Our Hope

Depending on His Promises

O Joy that seekest me through pain,
I cannot close my heart to thee;
I trace the rainbow thro' the rain,
And feel the promise is not vain
That morn shall tearless be.

George Matheson (1842–1906)
Albert L. Peace (1844–1912)

"O Love That Wilt Not Let Me Go"
Baptist Hymnal, © 1956 Convention Press, Nashville, TN

To Tie My Son's Shoes

*"Faith goes up the stairs that love has made
and looks out of the windows which hope has opened."*
Charles Haddon Spurgeon

A mother sees her son in a new light.

As I knelt to tie his shoes, I willed back the threatening tears. Memories flooded my mind as the 10½ tan casuals became, once again, the tiny white high-tops of 20 years earlier.

How I had enjoyed the busy, growing years with our two boys. I had always tried to protect them from hurt, from teaching playground safety rules in the early days to teaching safe driving habits when the time came. Now this son, our firstborn, had been hurt. How seriously, we didn't know. We would know later that day.

The accident last month had been traumatic, as accidents always are. The storm window had splintered and punctured his wrist. The night it happened, Randy walked into the den while applying pressure to the injury with a towel. "Mother," he said quietly, "you might want to call the emergency room."

A week later when the doctor removed the stitches, the damage was discovered. The accident had severed the tendon to the right index finger—the finger now flopped uncontrollably.

Moreover, there was serious nerve and tendon damage affecting the strength of his entire right hand.

Within a few days a specialist performed microsurgery in an attempt to rejoin the severed tendons. (Time alone would be required to repair the nerve damage.) With his arm in a cast shaped like a gigantic rabbit's paw, Randy came home to mend.

While he was incapacitated, we had long talks—the kind we used to have. We discussed his hopes, his plans for the future. Having just completed the long haul of college, he yearned to get his career underway; he disliked having to be away from the desk of his new accounting job. He regretted that now he could not take the state examination for Certified Public Accountant as scheduled that month—he had already paid his fee and had invested many hours in concentrated study. But his disappointment over this delay never gave way to bitterness.

Even more disturbing than the delays was the question of whether or not he would regain use of his right hand. His livelihood depended on that hand. His relaxing times at the piano depended on that hand. Fear must surely have gnawed at him as it did me. But there was no fuming, no fretting.

Now the day had come to learn whether or not the surgery had been successful. His shoes tied, Randy asked, "Do you think you can drive me to Emory Hospital OK?"

"Oh, sure," I answered, perhaps too quickly, trying to sound more confident than I felt. We crawled into the family car and headed for the Connector, then onto I-85 South for the 50 miles to Atlanta where the specialist would remove the cast.

Randy was accustomed to driving in heavy traffic; I wasn't. But he didn't nag me for going too slowly, or for failing to pass another car when it was the logical thing to do. If my driving made him nervous, he didn't show it. When finally we pulled into the parking space high on the deck at the hospital, I was undone. But not he.

I sat in the waiting room while he disappeared into the inner chambers of that frighteningly huge hospital. What fate awaited him there? Would his hand be able to do what his mind told it to do? The surgeon had made no promises. "Please God, let it be all right," I prayed quietly.

Rather than staring at blank walls, I fished into my handbag for something to read. From among the assorted papers that seem to accumulate there, I retrieved a little pamphlet entitled: "The Fruit of the Spirit." Opening it, I began to read, "But the fruit of the Spirit is love, joy, peace, patience ..." (Galatians 5:22, NASB).

Patience, I repeated to myself as my eyes studied the path down the hall which Randy had just taken. *Patience,* I said again as the message began to sink in. *Of course, that's it! That explains Randy's frame of mind during this whole ordeal. That explains his calmness. He's just been exercising his faith by allowing the Holy Spirit to help him.*

Thankfulness welled up within me. I suddenly realized that although I could no longer protect him as when he was little, God was with him all the time in the person of the Holy Spirit. From the time when, as a young boy, Randy accepted Jesus Christ as his Savior, this divine Helper had been teaching him, guiding him, strengthening him. I saw my son in a new light that day.

Randy strode through the door, this time with his arm in a somewhat less-restricting cast. He grinned as he announced, "It worked. I could move my finger."

Soon he would be able to tie his own shoes again.

Peril on Pine River

As written for: Mark"Izzy" Ismond

But now, Lord, what do I look for?
My hope is in you.
Psalm 39:7 NIV

Anticipation ran high that February afternoon as the three of us unloaded our canoes and camping gear. From high on the snow-covered ridge, we could hear the rushing water of Pine River in the valley below. Here in northern Michigan, Pine River was the only one still open—others were already frozen over.

I took a moment to breathe it all in. *Ah, yes. This is my kind of living—snow falling, temperature hovering at 20 degrees, and the river beckoning. It doesn't get much better than this.*

My fellow adventurers on this trip stood admiring the scene—hills covered with more than a foot of snow and as far as you could see, trees draped in white. Don and Jason, both nineteen, were members of the youth group I led. "Man, this is going to be great!" exclaimed Don, always ready for anything.

"Yeah, Iz," serious-minded Jason added. "Thanks for letting us come with you."

"No problem," I said. "I'm glad you two are interested. Not many people want to brave the elements this time of year." I realized I had quite a responsibility here. Don had canoed some; however, not in frigid conditions. Jason, although a good athlete, was not too comfortable on water. Even so, as an experienced canoeist and a triathlete myself, I felt confident I could handle anything that came up. The possibility of my being *over*-confident never entered my mind.

"Okay, you guys," I told the eager pair, "now the fun begins. It'll take several trips to get our supplies ferried down to the river." I left them working while I drove my 4-wheel drive to the parking area down around Low Bridge, the distance I estimated we could paddle in three days. By the time I hitchhiked back a couple of hours later, Don and Jason were waiting with canoes packed.

"Good job, you two," I said. "Let's get started. We can paddle an hour before dark." I could hardly wait for them to experience the awesome silence of winter in the woods. No people, no bugs, no bears ... In our green canoes, drifting along in calm water, we became so much a part of the picture the deer didn't even notice. They came right up to the river's edge to drink.

"Remember the rules of the wilderness?" I asked as we set up camp that night.

"How could we forget?" they said, laughing. "You've told us enough times. Then in unison they recited: "Water, shelter, fire, food—in that order."

"Well, we've got plenty of snow to drink for water," I said, then added, "and plenty of snow for shelter."

"*Snow* for shelter?" exclaimed Don. "Where is our tent!?"

"Tents are no good in this kind of weather," I explained. "Besides we're learning to be survivalists, remember? We'll build ourselves a snow cave. Grab something to help shovel." We piled up a small mountain of snow, stomped on it, let it harden thirty minutes, then scooped it out. Pleasantly surprised by the outcome, they proclaimed "It's an igloo!"

In that spirit of roughing it, we gathered branches and bark off the trees to put under our sleeping bags. The same source furnished firewood. By the time darkness closed in, we pulled out of the now hot coals our foil-wrapped meals. The aroma and taste of sausage, potatoes, and onions made all the work worthwhile.

By then it was 10 degrees. Even so, the guys were dubious about sleeping inside the snow cave, fearing it would collapse on us during the night. The following morning when we broke camp, I told Jason, "OK, smash in the snow cave." They both walked on top of it, and it stood. They couldn't believe it.

With their being properly impressed by our successful first day, I was feeling rather smug. Sometimes that can be a risky attitude when you are in the wild.

That second day started off well enough. Wearing several layers of thick clothing and heavy boots against the bitter cold, we stowed all our gear in the canoes and shoved off. Don and Jason shared a canoe, with Don at the bow. I paddled solo.

"Watch out for deadfalls," I reminded them. "In summer, the liveries clean out the fallen trees, but no such service in the winter. And remember what I taught you about running the rapids. We'll hit some pretty good ones."

They did fine all day—in spite of the temperature's never getting out of the low teens, with snow getting heavier and wind stronger. A couple of hours before dark, I drifted ahead to find a campsite, intending to keep the boys in view behind me. I had just rounded a curve when all of a sudden I sensed, *Something's wrong.* I back paddled, eddied, waited five or ten seconds. *They should be here by now.* Still certain I could handle any problem, I said a quick conversational prayer, "Lord, this could get interesting." I whipped around and started paddling up stream.

As I got around the bend, there on the steep side of the river was Jason, soaking wet. On the opposite side, on a narrow flat area, stood a drenched Don. They were running down, gesturing wildly, shouting. Following their flailing arms, I spotted their canoe that now was under four feet of ice-encrusted water.

Hypothermia can set in within minutes at this temperature, my mind said. *It can quickly prove fatal.* I noted that the steep hill behind Don's position would give some protection from the fierce wind. *Somehow I must get Jason to the other side in a hurry!*

Jason, meanwhile, was trying to walk out on a floating logjam, hollering, "I've got to get in your canoe!" *He's looking to jump in my canoe! Water's flowing under those logs! He could sink us both!*

"Go back, Jason," I yelled. "I can't get you here. I'll come around and get you."

But Jason, near panic, came running back out the logjam, and fell on one of the logs. *I'll have to risk it.* I let my canoe drift over and he jumped in while I fought mightily to keep us from tipping. Even so, my canoe took on water.

Now I had my fully loaded canoe— in which I was sitting in the middle—plus a 175-lb. panic-stricken man, with lots of heavy wet clothing and no paddle. With a second man waiting on the opposite shore, both of them in danger of hypothermia, their extra clothes now under water. My mind raced, *If I go under trying to get us across, my dry clothes will be gone, too. Then what will we do?*

That's when I knew I needed help from a higher power. I said, "Lord, this one is in your hands. I'm not sure I'm even thinking clearly. Whatever happens, I've got to lean totally on you."

Somehow, I got us over there and Jason scrambled ashore. They were already getting sluggish, not able to concentrate. *I've got to hurry! And I've got to keep them moving!* I motioned toward the only accessible trees, "You guys gather some firewood—bark, branches."

From the canoe I retrieved my duffel bag. *Good! It's still dry*. I fished out my tarp. Set up a windbreak. Started dolling out warm clothes and boots from my personal gear. *I hope I brought enough for both*. With a lot of improvising, like wool socks for Jason's gloves, I got them covered in *something*. Then started them on water and raisins, dried tangerines and grapes while I got the fire up. They seemed to be responding.

But the temperature was diving toward zero as wind whipped the snow to almost blizzard condition, and darkness was rapidly closing in. With just the tarp and one sleeping bag, I knew we had to get out of there. I wasn't sure of our location, but I figured we were five or six miles from a road with possibly another six miles to my truck. Considering the deep snow and dense forest, it was hardly a night for hiking. I was already weary from a day of paddling and the stress of the rescue. *Can I get to our vehicle and back in time?* I had to try.

With the three of us hovering around the fire, I said, "Don." "Jason." They looked up. "I'm going for the truck so we can get you some place warm." They nodded. "It might take me a long while, but I'll be back. Keep the fire going and remember to drink water and eat."

Taking a compass reading, I headed off into the night. It took twenty minutes just to get up the steep, heavily forested hills from the river basin. Then, wonder of wonders, at the top of the third bluff was a snowmobile trail. I followed it, leaving sticks for markers to help find my way back. Alternately I ran twenty minutes, then walked twenty, thankful for my training as a long-distance runner.

After three and a half hours, sweaty and chilled, I became frantic. *I've been gone too long! I need to get back!* "Lord, are you still helping?"

When at last I made it, I found Don and Jason standing in the pitch dark. They had let the fire go down and had quit taking water or food. Jason was shivering, his condition precarious. I realized just how weak they had become when we started to the truck. Much younger than I, they couldn't make it up the steep hills without my help.

Once inside the Pathfinder, I thought we were home free. "All we need now is a warm motel room, hot shower, and bed," I said.

We pulled into Cadillac, Michigan, about eleven o'clock at night, only to find the town booked up. The heavy snowfall had brought in all the skiers. "Lord, what am I going to do now?"

Into my mind popped a thought. *The family of a friend from Grand Rapids has a cottage in this area!* Several long distance calls later, I located his brother in Indiana. "Izzy," he said, "if you need the cottage, it's yours. Funny thing, we haven't had time to come up and close it for the winter. This is the first year we've left the heat and water on."

As it turned out, the cottage was just three miles from where we were at the moment. In the warm cottage, we found food on the shelves and bottled water in the refrigerator. "Lord. I wouldn't have known to even ask for all this. Thank you, thank you."

After two days there recovering from our ordeal, we headed home. And stopped for ice cream, of all things. Over a chocolate sundae I said, "Do you guys realize how close we came?"

"Man, that was great!" answered happy-go-lucky Don. "I want to go again."

Jason, on the other hand, was not eager to repeat the experience. I asked him, "Were you praying? Were you asking God for help?"

"No," he said, "I knew you would take care of us. My faith was in *you.*"

My jaw dropped. "Jason, I've got to tell you, I put all *my* faith in the Lord. I'll admit, it takes a while for an adventurer to ask for help. But when you jumped in my canoe, I sent up an urgent prayer, 'I'm over my head here, Lord,' and I didn't mean just the water. 'I can't handle this on my own; it's all in your hands.'"

Both boys listened intently. "Jason," I said, "you were being held, not by me, but by the Lord."

All fell silent. After several moments, I added, "Guys, our crisis taught me an important truth. No matter how skilled I am, how confident, or how well prepared, there are times when I'll need help from a higher power."

More silence as we stood to get our heavy jackets. "Want to know what else I learned," I asked, "something powerful?"

"Sure, Iz," they said, almost in unison, "What's that?"

"When I do call on God for help," I told them, "He's always listening."

One stressful time of crisis, seasons came and went, but I barely saw them. Then one glorious day, Spring erupted, full bloom, as if just for me. This poem (p.131) resulted. As encouragement in your own time of crisis, I share it now along with God's promise: "Weeping may endure for a night, but joy comes in the morning" (Psalm 30:5b, NKJV).

After Winter — Spring

—Gloria Cassity Stargel

Oh, the beauty of it all! Spring!
When God reaffirms His promise to us,
After cold, dark days of winter
Come warm, light days of spring.

Spring—when nature is awakening
And tiny green buds are making leaves;
Jonquils smile brightly, while
Hyacinths burst forth to greet the sun;
Forsythia cascades in golden profusion and
Spirea dons long boughs of lacy snow.

Tulip trees, resplendent now, clasp hands with
Crabapples and Weeping Cherries,
Though Dogwoods and Azaleas wait impatiently
To take their place in the splendor.

The skies seem more brilliant, the sunsets—Transcendent.
The Great Master Painter dips His brush
And with giant strokes—illumines the Universe!
The oranges and blues blend into soft, soft shades of
    purple—
Ever changing their kaleidoscope of colors—
Mirroring in the water until the lake itself is orange glass.
And mirroring to this renewed soul that

Beauty—and Hope—still abide.

When Prayers Take Twists and Twines

As written for: Regina Hines

Delight yourself in the Lord, and He will give you the desires of your heart.
Psalm 37:4, NIV

It is said, "Money doesn't grow on trees." Yet for this Mom, God shows her it *can.*

Kudzu. The vine Southerners love to hate! I well recall the day when first we met. The scorned plant didn't look anything like prayer-answering material. Certainly not *mine.*

I was visiting my Alabama sister-in-law that November. "Regina, come on out in the backyard," she said, heading out the screen door. "Let me show you what that nuisance is doing to our garden."

There, threatening to engulf the patch of ground where rows of snap beans and okra once grew, were huge heart-shape-leafed vines, vines that twisted and lapped over one another, turning in all directions. Tentacles, green in season, already had gobbled up sections of cultivated soil like some hungry beast. Dormant

132

now and brown, the vines had consumed acres of land, covering the rolling countryside as far as eye could see.

"What*ever* is *that?*" I exclaimed.

"That, Regina, is *kudzu,*" she explained, "our nemesis in the South. It was first brought here from Japan to help soil erosion. Well, it keeps our red hills from washing away alright," she said. "Trouble is, it doesn't know when to quit. It is completely out of control.

"Is it good for anything else?" I wondered.

"Not as far as I'm concerned," she said, disgustedly. "To me it is utterly useless."

Useless. I understood that term well enough. That's the way I had been feeling lately, especially since I learned my adult daughter needed additional funds for advanced education and I couldn't help her. *Why didn't I train for something productive?* I often asked myself.

Of course, for years, rearing five children was more than a full-time job. When I finally had free time, I enjoyed my hobby of arts and crafts. But now, like those kudzu vines, I seemed to be taking from life without giving anything back. *Lord, I'd really like to help my daughter. Would you please show me a way?*

Meanwhile, in Alabama that day, my sister-in-law was saying, "Kudzu is like a hibernating bear. Quiet now. But just wait until it comes to life in the spring." She paused, clearly exasperated. "It will devour anything that stands still—trees, power lines, old cars, barns, even houses! Sometimes, at eighteen inches a day, you can almost *see* it growing. And you can hardly kill the stuff!"

Almost as a dare, I flippantly offered: "Let's gather some of it. I'll make you a Christmas wreath."

She was less than enthusiastic about the prospect, but we wrestled a few tenacious tendrils out of the ground. I set up a chair out in the sunshine and began pulling off leaves. Working with the stubborn stems, I wondered how I'd ever make *anything* out of kudzu.

After I got the vines somewhat pliable, though, I began bending and twisting them into a rather lop-sided wreath. The more I looked at it, the more I realized it had *character*. I tucked in a sprig of holly, attached a red bow, and my sister-in-law *loved* her one-of-a-kind Christmas wreath!

Intrigued, when I got back home to Georgia, I began looking around *my* area for kudzu. I didn't need to look far. Kudzu twists and twines its way over a large part of the state. Often it creates an animal-shaped sculpture as it drapes itself over trees and bushes.

As a transplanted Northerner, I had heard of the plant, yet knew little of its history. And I couldn't find anyone around who had tried using it for crafts. The day I hauled in a batch of kudzu and dumped it onto our carport, my husband just shook his head. "Sweetheart," he said, "What in the world are you doing?"

"I'm going to try weaving a basket out of this," I answered, trying to sound more optimistic than I felt. "I might even sell a few."

"It'll never work," he insisted. "And even if it did, folks in the south will laugh. They are not about to let you put any of that hated vine inside their homes. It's bad enough what it's doing on the *outside*."

Stubborn as kudzu, I fashioned a basket. My first handiwork was so bad I burned it.

Undaunted, throughout the year I took out my frustrations, my feelings of inadequacy, by arguing with that aggravating vine, the rough texture often making my hands bleed. By trial and error, I learned the best time to harvest the vines was early spring or late fall and those growing up tree trunks were both easier to harvest as well as cleaner. I found the vines underneath the top layer proved more flexible and the larger vines proved more durable.

I persevered, for by then I was mesmerized by kudzu with a beauty all its own—both growing green in uncontrolled formations and in the antique sheen and delightful markings of the vines when dried.

Due to the interesting if often grotesque shapes of the knotty vines, I chose to weave baskets in free form, letting the kudzu go pretty much where it wanted to, which, of course, is its nature. I just coaxed it into forms resembling baskets—each with its own personality.

I learned that leaving tiny roots on the finished product gives a special, softening effect. I tried splitting the vine, dipping it in dye wash, and coming up with gorgeous, subdued colors. Some baskets I braided with eucalyptus—on wreaths I began adding ribbon and other custom trimming. Often, along with the kudzu, I'd weave and twine honeysuckle, wisteria and wild grape, giving additional texture.

During all those hours I spent weaving, I continued to talk with God about my daughter's financial need and my feeling of failure. Still, I thanked Him daily for this therapeutic hobby for by then I had learned to love working with the vines.

Finally, when I had several baskets ready, I bravely placed a small ad in an antique catalog, of all places. The owner of a little shop in a neighboring city read the ad and, sight unseen, phoned in an order for two dozen baskets! I never bought another ad because word spread like kudzu—someone had finally found a use for the pest.

Through our crafts, kudzu and I both gained new self-respect. For in spite of all our blemishes, varied shapes and stubborn ways, with God's help we were contributing something useful, something even beautiful.

Soon I phoned my daughter, "Go ahead and enroll in graduate school. I have funds enough for the first quarter. We'll trust God for the rest."

The old adage says, "Money doesn't grow on trees." Yet in my case, at least, God answered a mother's prayer by letting it do exactly that. And my daughter earned her Master's Degree in Nursing on what we call a "kudzu scholarship."

Surprising things can happen when prayers take twists and twines.

⚓

NOTE: Regina Hines is dubbed the "Kudzu Artist of North Georgia." Often working with decorators, her baskets, wreaths, mirror frames, and window treatments grace the walls and floors of fine homes and restaurants throughout the country.

Ready!

"Be ye therefore ready also; for the Son of man cometh at an hour when ye think not."
Luke 12:40, KJV

A Devotional

Three off-duty firemen were painting our house. One day, the dispatcher at our local fire station phoned. "Mrs. Stargel," she said, "please tell the men we have a big fire at the American Legion Home. We need them."

I hurried the message to the painters. Instantly, the three men—firemen now—scampered off ladders, placed their brushes into cans of paint, hastily wrapped each with a cloth, piled into their van, and were gone. *Snatched away.*

I stood alone in a world that now was eerily silent. It seemed as if those painters had never been there at all. Yet, I saw evidence of the last stroke of a brush and paintbrush handles stuck out of opened cans of paint.

I returned to my desk lost in thought. What a vivid reminder of that scene in the Bible of Jesus' return to earth: "… the one shall be taken, and the other left" (Luke 17:35 KJV).

I spoke aloud to the empty house, "For sure I don't want to be the one left behind." Probably, I sounded a little flippant; but in my heart I was quite serious. I determined immediately: *I'll try to stay "prayed up," as they say, so I'll be ready.*

Lord Jesus, remember me when You come to claim your own.

Flight for Freedom

As written for: Oscar T. Cassity, Major, U.S.A.F. Retired

*"Man's most precious possession,
second only to life itself, is freedom."*
Col. Ben Purcell, former POW

Could he rescue them all? He had to try.

Barely 20 years old, I was a new Air Force pilot serving in Europe during World War II. Orders came for me to fly into Yugoslavia—behind enemy lines—and rescue a group of twenty-six displaced persons of several nationalities, including some Americans, who had been hiding for months—in basements, in barns, in woods. They were now in the custody of a few friendly German officers who somehow had contacted our security, requesting help.

Orders further stated that there would be no airport available. And, of course, it was necessary that I fly in undetected or get shot down. For those reasons, I was to take the absolutely smallest plane that would do the job.

The day of the mission, I reached the target area and landed on the designated tiny plot of pasture. Only to be greeted by—not twenty-six refugees—but *forty* desperate souls—all ages, few speaking English.

A quick prayer went up, *Lord, what to do?* I simply did not have space for forty. Yet, they faced almost certain death from starvation and untreated health problems, or from the Nazi forces, should they be discovered. I couldn't bear to leave even one behind.

I told a couple of our crew: "Estimate the weight of each person and add them up. We'll factor in the weight of our remaining fuel and determine if our aircraft can get off the ground if we take them all." The fact that the refugees were undernourished—and therefore very thin—was to their advantage right then.

We pushed the limit. I had them sitting in the aisle, three abreast, with orders, "Do *not* move."

Finally loaded, we rolled down the short, grassy makeshift airstrip, straining mightily to gain the optimum 100 knots for take off. "40 knots, Sir," my co-pilot called out. "50 knots." "60 knots." Trees at the end of the runway loomed dead ahead. At 80 knots, I dropped the quarter flap and forced the plane up, my landing gear brushing the tops of the trees.

When we reached 6,000 feet, I went back to tell our passengers, "We're out!"

A sea of faces smiled broadly.

Tears rolled down cheeks.

No doubt prayers of thanksgiving went up.

But not one person moved. Not even an inch.

During the following years in my military career, I experienced many hair-raising missions—combat flights in Europe and Korea, tight flights for the Berlin Airlift, unique flights to the South Pole—missions that required, and received, help from a Higher Power. Yet, that memorable moment aboard the little packed plane remains one of the most satisfying. I can still see those forty expressions—expressions that proclaimed louder than words—the absolute joy—of—*freedom.*

The Day My Son Became a Marine

"What time I am afraid, I will trust in thee."
Psalm 56:3, KJV

A mother learns to let go—and let God.

"Bye, Mom," Rick said as he quickly planted a kiss on my cheek and gave me one last firm hug.

"Bye, Son," I managed, then watched him fold his broad-shouldered, six-foot frame into his friend's tiny, green sports car. *I will not cry*, I told myself. *Not until he's out of sight.*

I think I had dreaded this day ever since he was born—this day when our last child would leave home. That he should be going into military service caused even more gnawing fear.

He wouldn't let me go see him off at the airport. "No emotional scenes, please." *I'll stay busy*, I told myself. *Try not to think.* No matter. My eyes kept glancing at the clock. Was it time yet for Flight 304? At the appointed hour, I could stand it no longer.

Running by the closet, I grabbed my heavy coat and hurried out into the backyard. We're only 50 miles from Atlanta International. *Maybe I can see his plane from here.* I realized I

141

probably couldn't. But I just had to try. I yearned for one more glimpse, even though from 20,000 feet.

I raced down the hill behind the house to a large clearing with a view of the sky in all directions. I barely noticed the near-perfect weather of an autumn afternoon. Instead I saw the old oak tree farther down in the backyard, looking forlorn, stripped now of its leaves.

I knew how the tree felt. A part of my life had just ended as I said goodbye to twenty-two years of happiness. My chest hurt so from the burden, I wondered if perhaps the heart *does* break at times.

While my ears strained for the sound of an airplane, thoughts of past, present, and future played leapfrog in my brain. *Where have the years gone?* I wondered. *Wasn't it just yesterday that we brought the blue bundle home from the hospital? Now he's going off to become a Marine Corps officer with all that implies.*

Yet, I kept seeing him as a curly-haired toddler with huge brown eyes shining in a cherubic face, all love and innocence. *By training him to fight, will they destroy all the tenderness that I've nurtured?*

Anyway, it's not fair, I grumbled. I wanted him to grow up to be independent, and I'm proud of his willingness to serve his country. But I didn't want him to go so far from home. *You do a good job as a parent and you put yourself right out of business.*

Tortured with these conflicting sentiments, I shrank from this day. Now it had arrived and I stood searching the sky. Only a few clouds floated in the huge expanse. I clutched my coat tighter around the neck as the chilly air signaled the coming of winter, both to nature and to me.

Dear Jesus, help me, I sobbed, grasping for the comfort I had learned to expect from my faith. *Take away this awful pain.*

The distant drone of a jet engine broke my reverie. *There it is! That must be it! Rick's plane. It's climbing and heading north.*

Then, just as suddenly as it appeared, it slid into the heavens, out of sight. He was out there alone somewhere ...

I stared at the vacated space in the sky. *Good-bye, Son. Good-bye.*

Reluctantly I trudged back into the house, pleading, *Dear God, You tell us in your Word to cast all our cares upon you because you care for us.[1] So, Lord, here, I give You my burden. I can't carry it alone.*

But after I gave God my burden, I took it right back. I forgot all about the message in the great old hymn "Take your burden to the Lord and leave it there."

Instead, the next day I was back in the grips of deep sorrow and self-pity. I refused to clean Rick's room until his dad could be in there with me. I avoided the quiet radio workbench and the weights stacked neatly in the basement. I found myself unable to do anything constructive.

Rather, I walked from room to room, tears coursing down my cheeks. It was more than pain of separation. I sensed that Rick could never be the same; and my grief for that loss was wrenching, tearing.

Late that afternoon, I found myself standing at the kitchen window, gazing out at another afternoon sky. I don't know how long I stood there, lost in memories. But finally my eyes again focused on the old oak tree in the backyard. With its bare branches it looked as sad as I felt.

But this time I saw something I hadn't seen before, Those bare branches reached expectantly upward, confident of new life next spring. They presented a picture of faith, of trust. I felt a surge of hope, for it was as if God himself had shown me

---

1   1 Peter 5:7, KJV

that picture when I needed it most. Surely I had known that I could trust my son to God. And that I could trust God to heal my hurt. Had I failed to reach up to Him, in trust?

Forgive me, Lord, I prayed as I bowed my head and my heart before Him. *Teach me, once more, to trust you in all things.*

A calmness filled my consciousness as I gradually yielded to our Lord's tender care. Finally I could add the close to my prayer. *Now, God, I turn Rick over to You. I guess, really, You had him all the time, didn't You? Thank you, Father, for those beautiful twenty-two years.*

Once again I studied the old oak tree down the hill. Now we had even more in common, that old tree and I. For I, too, reached expectantly upward and my burden felt strangely lightened. And though the tears were still in my eyes, I knew that this, too, would pass. That tomorrow—or the next tomorrow—I would smile again.

At last, across the miles, I whispered my benediction: "Good-bye, my son. Goodbye. May God, who loves you, hold you in the palm of His hand."

And I knew now that He would. Yes, God would take care of Rick. And me.

I had learned—once again—that faith means trust.

Package Deal

As written for: Diane Dwyer

But I will hope continually,
and will yet praise thee more and more.
Psalm 71:14, KJV

Homeless, once again—yet, her hope and faith live on.

On that overcast October afternoon, I looked plenty pitiful. Standing at the barn beside my beat-up little travel trailer, with no car to pull it; my horse, with no trailer to transport him; and four trusting dogs, expecting me to feed them—I presented a sad sight. But we came as a package deal, and that day, there were no demands for package deals.

In the past I had asked God to lead me, and I tried to follow. But now doubts piled on top of one another; I had lost yet another job. Clearly, something was wrong. *Lord, have I chosen the wrong line of work?*

I had been living in a furnished mobile home on a large farm where I trained and cared for 30 horses and all that goes with that job. I love working with horses—having devoted 45

145

years to it—but the work had become too hard for one person to handle.

I dutifully wrote my employer a thirty-day notice of resignation. When I delivered the message, without warning harsh words flew, ending with my being told, "You are leaving *now!*"

Leaving! Where in the world will I go? I had counted on using those thirty days to train someone to take my place and to locate a new home for my "family." With my two sons grown and living away, that family now consisted of my sweet horse and four wonderful dogs—almost as precious to me as my children.

My furry family stood there now, looking to me for answers: princely Swift Viking, my dark brown appendix quarter horse with the nickname of Vi-Guy; three bassets—Lovey, a retired show dog; Lamar and Andrew, foster children I adopted from the Bassett Hound Rescue; and Rudy, the precious miniature dachshund I saved from almost certain euthanasia—having brought him home in a borrowed doggy wheelchair.

"Don't you worry, Vi-Guy," I said, stroking the white star on his forehead. "We'll find you a wonderful pasture, with a stream, and a nice warm barn. Just you wait and see."

"And you guys," I said, kneeling down to hug the canine quartet surrounding me, demanding attention. "We'll be OK. I know we will."

But on the inside, at that moment, I wondered if, when, and how I could fulfill those promises.

Besides, I knew there loomed an even larger problem. I faced some serious soul searching. *I know the questions I'll get from my children. "Mother, why don't you get a real job? One that pays better. One with some security?"*

I'd heard it all before. Even from friends.

It all ran through my mind as I stood there in a daze. *My plants and memorabilia—where will I put them? Where will I hang my clothes? And what about my family!* "Lord," I cried out, "I need your help here, real bad."

I phoned the teacher of my new Bible Study Class and shared my plight. "I'll be over in the morning to get your plants and care for them," she offered. "How else can I help?"

A few minutes later, a member of the class called. "Tomorrow I'll canvass stores in town for cardboard cartons to help you pack," she said.

Around 9:30 that night a young man, who boarded his horse at the farm, knocked on my door. His mother was with him. "We want to help you," she said. "We know what it's like to be without a home. Ours burned earlier this year. You can park your trailer in our yard until you decide what to do."

Next morning, another boarder said, "I have an empty pasture. I'll keep Vi-Guy for you."

Still another one heard that conversation. "Vi-Guy will be lonely all by himself. I'll take my two donkeys out there to keep him company."

I couldn't believe the kindness of these people! Tears threatened to spill down my face when yet another boarder said, "Let me take your dogs to the kennel for a few days while you relocate. I'll pay the bill."

In spite of rain that lasted days, I managed to get my meager belongings into storage and prepare for the move. The hardest part was saying goodbye to Vi-Guy, knowing I couldn't see him often. Wearing a downcast face he leaned over, nudged me, and closed his eyes for my kiss. "I'll come get you, Vi," I said, giving him one last hug, "just as soon as I can."

Through it all, every Sunday I attended the Bible Study Class and reported on my progress, or lack of it. The members encouraged me, prayed regularly for me. And during those three months, I had many heart-to-heart talks with myself, and with the Lord.

In one of our conversations I prayed, *Lord, You know how much I love horses and being outdoors. But if I'm supposed to be doing something else, please lead me to it.* Then I added, *But, Lord, if I'm in the right field, please let me know it without a shadow of a doubt.*

About that time our entire church embarked on a forty-day study on finding your God-given purpose in life. Exactly what I needed. One day I felt the Lord say to me, "Be true to yourself, Diane."

And what is my true self? Then I answered my own question. My true self needs little in the way of "stuff." I need only food to eat and a safe place to sleep, friends who love me and animals that need me.

My true self loves horses; I have from the time I was a nine-year-old, horse-crazy child. I've never gotten over it. I even love barns—the warmth and the way light plays through the beams, changing throughout the day. I like the smell of fresh sawdust, the feel of breezes blowing through the wide center aisle.

I like the welcome I receive in the mornings when every horse puts his head over the front of the stall, waiting for a word—and breakfast—from me. I like the night sounds as the horses whinny to one another and the cows out in the pasture low softly.

And I'm good with animals. They *love* me. Who else serves them their hay with "Here is your salad course. What dressing would you like?" (They always choose "ranch.") After their entrée of oats, often they're offered dessert from the apple chunks in my pocket.

I enjoy training and grooming horses. They are my friends, each with its own personality. Later, when I get them all settled in for the night, it reminds me of that satisfied feeling when my boys were little and safely tucked in after a full day of play.

Besides, where else would I be considered Queen of the Castle, or in this case, the Barn? One of our young boarders always greeted me with an exaggerated bow and "Your Majesty."

I've held "real" jobs, but they just weren't me. I appreciate my sons' concern and that of my friends. I realize they had my interests at heart, and I love them for it. But I knew now that giving up the work I love was unthinkable.

Early one December morning, in my jacket pocket I felt a scrap of paper with a phone number I had hesitated to call all those weeks. An inner voice said, *It's time to call it, Diane.* Vickie Mead answered. "Why don't you come on over and talk with Brett?" she said.

"I'll be right there," I said and by 8:30 was turning into the entrance of picturesque Mountain Creek Ranch. I followed the gravel driveway as it curved around in front of the white-frame main house to reveal, amid the acreage in back, a beautiful barn surrounded by pastures with grazing horses and cattle, spectacular scenery, and even a mountain in the background.

A tour of the barn showed 16 stalls (one of them empty), a bunkhouse, kitchen, shower facilities, even an office—all needing someone to use them. *The answer to my prayers!* My mind raced. *Dare I hope?*

Brett Mead asked, "How soon can you be packed?"

"Give me a couple of hours," I answered.

"I'll bring the truck over to get you."

By noon my little trailer was snuggled against the side of that barn with a gorgeous view of wooded hills and mountain. Soon the dogs were exploring their new farm.

"Let's go get your horse," Brett said and off we drove, the horse trailer bouncing along behind us.

When Vi-Guy heard us coming, his head sprang up and he beat us to the gate. "I told you I was coming back, Vi," I said hugging his neck and kissing his nose. "Just wait until you see our new home!"

When we reached Mountain Creek, I put him in the paddock so he could look around and meet the other horses. Right away he found the creek and played in it like a child on its first day of summer vacation.

It's springtime now—a bright, warm afternoon. Birds sing their little hearts out, busy building nests. With their cheerful background music, I'm eating supper sitting beside my tiny trailer, now cozy as a cocoon. Nearby, Vi-Guy munches grass and the "boys" play at my feet. My eyes rest on the peaceful scene of rolling pasture edged with trees sporting new green leaves, and beyond that—a sunset's purple haze silhouettes Long Mountain.

I couldn't be more content. For this is the real me. And I believe this is exactly where God wants me to be at this moment in time.

Do I have any guarantees about tomorrow? No. But I'm confident God knows and cares about my welfare. And that is enough.

So take another look. You'll see one happy camper. Make that six happy campers—Vi-Guy, Lovey, Andrew, Lamar, Rudy—and *me*.

Yes, God is good.

Life is good.

Crisis On The Court

*"Cast all your anxiety on Him,
because He cares for you."*
1 Peter 5:7, NIV

A mother hears from God.

July 25 was hot and humid at Parris Island Marine Recruit Depot in South Carolina where our younger son, Rick, was competing in the Marine East Coast Championship Tennis Tournament.

Rick's dad and I, along with his brother, Randy, had determined this would be a splendid time to vacation at our favorite spot—Hilton Head Island, a short drive from Parris Island. We could watch Rick's matches. And, when he wasn't playing tennis, he could spend time with us at the beach.

That morning, in our rented condo on Hilton Head, Rick gathered his tennis rackets and utility bag. "Mom, are you coming over with Dad to watch today's matches?"

"Matches!" I exclaimed. "You mean you're playing more than *one*? In this *heat*?"

"Yep," he said, giving me a big bear hug. "Doubles this morning and singles this afternoon."

I returned his hug. "I think I'll stay here where it's cool. But I'll be there for the finals tomorrow, so hang in there!"

Then I added the standard reminder of parents everywhere, "Drive carefully."

Rick didn't know the real reason I was staying behind. Today was his birthday and I planned to surprise him with an old-fashioned, home-cooked meal—something he missed in the Corps. I'd brought along all his favorite foods, even a chocolate layer cake.

First I reconnoitered the little condo and located a set of peach-colored straw place mats for the table along with a basket of seashells that would make a fine centerpiece. All afternoon I spent in the tiny kitchen, preparing a feast. I hummed a happy tune. Yes, all was well with my world. Or so I thought.

I had just turned the fried chicken when Randy came in from a swim. "Smells good," he said. "Let me take a quick shower and I'll set the table."

"Great," I answered. "Everything's just about ready. They should be here soon."

Now, two hours later, I was trying to keep dinner from drying out as my eyes kept darting toward the kitchen clock. Randy headed back out the front door, trying without success to hide his own uneasiness. "I'll see if they're coming," he called over his shoulder.

By then, my mind had pictured all the worst possible scenarios of highway accidents. I had to *do* something. I cut off the burners on the stove and walked out onto the back deck. There, I leaned against the wood railing and stared into the shadows.

Beyond the sand dunes and sea oats silhouetted against the horizon, the Atlantic Ocean continued its rhythmic sway. Overhead, stars hung like millions of tiny lights in a black, velvet sky. *Surely,* I pondered, *God is all powerful, all loving, having made for us such a beautiful place.* And so I talked with Him there.

"Lord," I began, "please let Rick and Joe be safe ..." All at once, I was seized by a heavy feeling of regret. Regret that I hadn't prayed for them this morning—I just told them to be careful. And now, maybe, it was too late to pray. "Forgive me, Lord."

After some while, the answer came. As softly as the ocean breeze caressing my cheek, I sensed God say to me, "Gloria, I knew what you meant this morning when you said, 'Be careful.' What *I* heard was, 'God go with you and protect you.' Remember, Gloria, *I* know the heart."

My concern lightened, I hurried back inside, and once more, warmed up dinner. "Randy, get ready to light the candles," I called out. "They'll be here soon and they'll be starved."

Within minutes, the door opened and the two of them trudged in—completely bedraggled. Joe carried Rick's tennis gear. Rick stood there, pale and exhausted, clutching around his wet clothes a blue sheet stamped: U.S. NAVAL HOSPITAL.

"What in the world ..." was all I managed.

As I collapsed onto a chair and Rick, still wrapped in his sheet, folded into another, Joe recounted the events of their terrifying afternoon.

"The day turned out to be a scorcher with no sign of a breeze," he started. "Even where I stood in the shade of those ancient crape myrtle trees, the heat was oppressive. Rick and his partner had just won a hard-fought doubles match, and now Rick was in the second set of his singles match—had his opponent down 6-4, 5-4. Suddenly, on the court, Rick screamed out in pain and fell to the asphalt surface, writhing in agony. Severe leg cramps.

"A nearby officer motioned to another Marine, 'Sergeant, drive Lt. Stargel over to the Bachelor Officer Quarters and get him under a cold shower right away.' They put Rick into a jeep and sped away. Pulse pounding, I jumped in our car and raced after them.

"At his quarters, as they helped Rick across the parking lot, a new wave of spasms struck, again knocking him to the steamy pavement. This time he appeared to be in serious trouble. Muscles knotted all over his body. One clamped like a vise on his chest. He had difficulty breathing. 'I need help,' he gasped.

"'Call the medics!' the sergeant shouted. Soon a military ambulance careened across the field and whisked Rick to the base hospital."

As Joe continued his story there in the condo, *I* could barely breathe. "In the emergency room," he said, "they plunged Rick into a tub of ice and water up to his chin, in an effort to lower his dangerously high temperature. They gave him shots; they forced liquids."

At this point, Rick joined in the telling. "All this time, Dad and several medics rubbed frantically as fresh cramps hit and I'd call out first one muscle, then another. Even the bottom of my feet cramped."

"His muscles became like granite until we rubbed them down," Joe added. "I worked feverishly and prayed silently, *Please, God, don't let a cramp hit his heart.*"

When, at long last, the pains had subsided and Rick's temperature returned to normal, the doctor explained that due to excessive perspiration, Rick had become gravely dehydrated, depleting essential elements in the blood, thus causing the cramping.

On top of that, his other symptoms indicated heatstroke—a critical emergency. Often fatal. The cramping might have saved his life because it resulted in his getting early medical treatment.

"Oh, by the way," Joe added, "the doctor said for Rick to eat a good meal tonight."

As the four of us gathered around that little table with the peach-colored mats and seashell centerpiece, the twenty-four candles on Rick's chocolate cake held special significance, a reminder that God watches over us day and night. Even under normal circumstances, when the four of us sit down for a meal, the smile on my face moves Rick to say, "Mother is like a Mama cat with her kittens, totally content only when all her little kittens are safe within reach."

It's true. And this time I didn't hesitate to pray aloud, thanking God for sparing Rick's life—for bringing us together as a family once again.

Then, I breathed yet another unspoken prayer. *Thank you, Lord, for knowing the hearts of Moms and Dads. When we say "Be careful," we really mean "God go with you and protect you."*

So it is when speaks the heart.

NOTE: The day after his crisis on the court, Rick and his partner won the Marine Corps East Coast Doubles Championship.

CHAPTER 5

Jesus, Our Lifeline

Marveling in His Miracles

As a mother stills her child,
Thou canst hush the ocean wild;
Bois-t'rous waves obey Thy will
When Thou say'st to them, "Be still;"
Wondrous Sov'reign of the sea,
Jesus, Saviour, pilot me.

Edward Hopper (1818-1888)
John E. Gould (1822-1875)

"O Love That Wilt Not Let Me Go"
Baptist Hymnal, © 1956 Convention Press, Nashville, TN

Her Angel Wore Hiking Boots

"Who does the best his circumstance allows does well;
acts nobly; angels could do no more."
—Edward Young,
Night Thoughts, *Night II*

An unlikely angel comes to the aid of an injured cheerleader.

That Sunday morning began at 5:00 A.M. for Haley Black, eighteen. *I'm glad I packed my bag last night,* she thought, still half asleep. *The vans leave the Athletic Center in thirty minutes.*

An upcoming freshman at West Georgia College in Carrolton, Georgia, Haley was excited about the trip to Myrtle Beach, South Carolina. This would be her first college-level cheerleading camp and the newly elected squad had practiced all summer. They were *ready*.

Pulling on shorts and tee shirt, socks and loafers, Haley combed her hair back into a ponytail, grabbed her bag, and was out the door. Nothing hinted that tragedy was about to invade her world.

Around the same time, in Marietta, Georgia, young Gary Willing, a musician in the Atlanta area, was also up at first light. In a small duffle bag, he stashed whatever he'd need for a couple nights back home in South Carolina.

Noting a chill in the air, Gary decided against his usual driving sandals. Instead, he retrieved from a drawer a new pair of yellow woolen socks, laced up his hiking boots, and bolted for the door. He'd promised his Mom he'd be in Columbia in time for lunch.

Heading his burgundy Pathfinder south, Gary stopped in Madison for a quick breakfast, set the cruise control and settled down for a long stretch on I-20.

At the college athletic center, the cheerleaders loaded into two vans. Haley's carried twelve girls plus the driver. Once underway, Haley kicked off her shoes and fell asleep. Blessedly, she didn't know when their van blew a tire and the vehicle flipped over and over in a violent crash. The impact hurled all thirteen passengers onto the unyielding pavement. When Haley briefly regained consciousness, she found herself sprawled, face down, on the yellow line in the center of a highway.

Unknowingly, Gary Willing was now driving down the same highway, just minutes behind the van filled with cheerleaders. With light early-morning traffic, he was relaxing with soft music from the tape deck when, upon cresting a hill, brake lights ahead in his lane startled him into alert status! A bus of some kind had stopped. And a car. *Oh, no, not a delay!* his thoughts ran. *I'll be late for lunch.*

As Gary got closer, he saw a van overturned and bodies— bleeding, broken, and bruised bodies—all over the road! Young people, it looked like, flung every which way! Almost by reflex, he reached for his cellular phone and hit **911**.

The dispatcher told him to drive on past the scene and report to her the mile marker so the emergency vehicles could locate the accident. Shaken, Gary sped up the road to the next marker. Having reported the number, hence the location, he desperately wanted to just keep going, his inner being saying, *I don't think I can face that sight again. Besides, I wouldn't know how to help.*

Agonizing with indecision, Gary turned off the interstate and pulled over. Gripping the steering wheel, he prayed, *Lord, what to do? Ask Mom,* came the answer. He dialed her number.

"Mom, it's horrible! It looks like a war movie!"

"Gary, you must go back."

"But Mom, what more can I do? I don't know any medical aid."

"Just *be* there for someone until an ambulance comes."

Down deep, Gary knew she was right. *Lord, please go with me.*

Turning the Pathfinder around, Gary raced back to the wreckage.

He stepped out into a nightmare. Fumes of hot radiator fluid hung low on the morning mist. An eerie silence enveloped all, even the bone-chilling groans. *Where to start? Lord, help!*

By now there were perhaps ten people on the scene, trying to administer what aid they could. Two military men in fatigues had IVs and were working with the most critically injured. Was Gary ever glad to see *those* guys.

Some girls were getting blankets out of another van. *Good idea,* Gary thought; *we need to keep the victims warm.* He chased over to help the girls. Frantic, they grabbed anything they could find—blankets, shirts, pillows …

Gary dreaded turning around. He pulled his faded-blue baseball cap down low on his face, attempting to shut out some of the view. Then, with arms full of makeshift bedding, he waded into the sickening scene. Hesitantly, he approached one victim at a time, draping each with the clothing items, trying to reassure those who were responsive.

He came to a young dark-haired woman, sprawled out on her stomach, straddling the centerline of the highway. Realizing that all she could see from that angle were his hiking boots, Gary crouched down on one knee. "Help will be here soon," he said, as he placed some covering on her. "You're gonna' be O.K."

She moaned.

"What happened?" he asked, sensing it important to keep her talking.

"I don't know," she managed. "Please don't leave me."

Then she said it again, "Please don't leave me."

So, Gary just lay down beside her, propping himself up on one elbow so she wouldn't have to strain to hear or see him. He began talking to her, trying to keep her calm. And trying to keep her from seeing what was going on all around her.

Gary remembered, from TV shows, that the victim must remain still until injuries can be evaluated, otherwise further damage, even death, can result. *This* injured one kept trying to get up. He patted her shoulder, "No, you must lie still."

"But I've got to get out of the road," she said. "I'll get run over." He assured her the traffic had been blocked; there was no danger of a car coming close. *I must get her mind on something else* he realized.

"What's your name? he asked.

"Haley," she managed. "Haley Black."

"Where are you from, Haley?"

"Gainesville, Georgia."

"Haley, would you like me to call your parents, to let them know you're alright?"

She blinked "yes," and mumbled the number. With a cell phone, Gary broke the news of an accident to her mom and dad. He assured them, "I'll stay with her until an ambulance comes."

"Tell Haley we're on our way," her dad said. "Please let us know where they take her."

It took twenty-five seemingly endless minutes for ambulances to arrive. Haley kept fading in and out of consciousness. To keep her awake, Gary asked about her school. Her boyfriend. Did she like music?

"My back hurts," she moaned, over and over. He told her that was a good sign, the fact that she could *feel.*

"I'm cold," she said, starting to shiver. Gary covered her free hand with his own, hoping to transmit heat and comfort.

At one point, she said, "My nose itches." *Oh, my, now what do I do?* he wondered. Ever so gingerly, he reached over and scratched Haley's nose.

Then she said, "My foot's cold. I don't know how I lost a sock."

Immediately Gary thought of the warm woolen socks he was wearing. *I might not have much to offer,* he told himself, *but here's something I can give.* He unlaced his hiking boots and pulled the yellow socks onto Haley's chilled feet.

At long last, EMTs were working with Haley, putting her into a body and neck brace, and strapping her onto a gurney. They rolled her over to the side of the road, along with two others of the injured, to wait for the next ambulance just as the first one roared away, siren blaring. Soon a helicopter landed and took one of those on the gurneys beside us.

Finally, an ambulance came for her. "Where are you taking her?" Gary shouted above the mass confusion.

"Wills," one EMT responded. "Wills Memorial Hospital. Washington, Georgia."

As the doors clanged shut, Gary called out, "I'll phone your parents, Haley."

Soon after, they airlifted Haley to Medical College of Georgia in Augusta.

The doctors first feared a broken neck, but further tests found she had suffered a chipped vertebra near the neck. But indeed her back was broken. Doctors closed her head wound with nine stitches, and there didn't seem to be lasting damage there.

On Tuesday, Gary returned to Georgia and drove down to the Augusta hospital. When he reached Haley's room, her family greeted him with hugs and tears, calling him "Haley's guardian angel."

Haley's mother overwhelmed Gary completely. "You probably saved Haley's life, Gary," she said. "The doctors tell us that if she had tried to get up out there on the highway, the results could have proved fatal, or could have paralyzed her for life!"

Gary stood there in awe as her mother continued, "As it is, she'll be in a cast—not allowed to walk—for several months, but after that, the doctors think she'll be just fine! We have *you* to thank for that, Gary." He could only shake his head in wonderment.

Gary walked over and took the hand of the pretty young lady trying to smile in spite of the neck brace and medication. He grinned back. "You're going to be OK, Haley. Thank, God, you're going to be OK."

"Thank you," she whispered, giving his hand a weak, but sincere squeeze.

While, in her heart, she added, "And thank *you*, God, for sending me an angel, an angel wearing hiking boots—and warm yellow socks."

ℳine Eyes Have Seen the Glory

"Who is this? Even the wind and the waves obey Him!"
Mark 4:41b, NIV

Released from death threat of cancer; a testimony of praise to The Father, Son, and Holy Spirit.

The Postman made his daily run about noon that Saturday. My husband stopped mowing the lawn and hurried to the mailbox. Coming into the kitchen where I was preparing lunch, Joe dropped the mail on the corner of the buffet—all except the small, white envelope.

As he reached for the letter opener, I reached for a towel to dry my hands. Gripping the 6 by 9 inch sheet of paper, Joe read aloud the report from his X-rays and lab tests.

"I think your doctor has dismissed you," I ventured.

"I think he has, too," Joe said, awe-struck.

"Read it again," I urged, trying to peer over his shoulder.

"There was no evidence of recurrent malignancy or other abnormalities," he repeated.

"You mean that's *it?*" I said. *No celebration? No fireworks? No bells ringing all over the world?* "You mean, we're free? We've been pardoned?"

Four years ago the medical world had agreed there was no hope for Joe's life. The cancer they discovered in his body was a fast-multiplying type with no known cure. "Most patients don't live more than six months," they said. Still, we dared ask God for a miracle.

The oncologist began last-ditch chemotherapy, trying to slow the progress of the disease. The radiologist followed with cobalt treatments. Both were terribly debilitating. It seemed that any living cells the disease didn't destroy, the treatments surely would. He was so sick that first year. So very sick.

Who can know the anguish of living four years under a death sentence! We had decided—without really saying so—to live each day to the fullest. Some days we could even forget it for a while. But, oh, the long nights. When fear crept in and faith faltered. Prayers often were wordless as we frantically clutched Jesus' hand.

But now! "No evidence of recurrent malignancy!" Praise God from whom all blessings flow! He made our cells and fashioned us in the first place; He holds the whole world in His hands; His love and grace are beyond all measure; He loved us enough to give His only begotten Son that we might have life eternal! This same Jesus, when He went back to Heaven to take His place beside the Father, sent the Holy Spirit to be our constant companion and guide!

Oh, for the words to honor Him. Oh, for the words to express the gratitude of our hearts. That He chose to bestow this miracle of life to us, His unworthy children. Hallelujah!

Thank you, heavenly Father. Thank you, blessed Jesus. Thank you, dear Lord, for loving us. Oh, dear Jesus, Thou who hast shown us thy glory, we give thee back our love, and our lives, forever.

AMEN

When healing has come.

O Blessed Warmth

I saw springtime today in all its glory
And its beauty warmed my soul.
It was different before.
You walked in shadow, so
I walked in shadow, too.
Strange—
When life hangs by a thread
The thread is all we see.
But today, I saw spring. Could it be?
Did He who made the stars
See our little thread
And from it weave
A Tapestry?
O blessed warmth.

—GCS

Rescue of Little Naomi

As written for: Mirna Whidden

Hush, my dear, lie still and slumber,
Holy angels guard thy bed.
Heavenly blessings without number
Gently falling on thy head.
Isaac Watts (1674-1748)
"A Cradle Hymn"

A tiny, two-year-old girl is lost overnight in the mountainous Chattahoochee National Forest. Throughout the world, people pray and wait.

Until my beeper sounded that November Friday afternoon, my major concern was getting home. An X-ray technician, I had just completed my shift at Union County Medical Center in Blairsville, Georgia, and started the hour-and-a-half drive. Darkness was closing in as I maneuvered my old Dodge Charger down the treacherous road around Blood Mountain.

Beep! My pager startled me. I answered to hear, "You're to call this number in Dahlonega."

168

"Dahlonega?" I wondered aloud, fear taking hold. Duane was taking the children hiking toward Dahlonega. But they should have been home hours ago!

I dialed the number. "LUMPKIN COUNTY SHERIFF'S OFFICE." Suddenly I felt sick to my stomach.

"This is Mirna Whidden," I said, panic building. "What's wrong?"

"You need to get down here right away."

I started to cry. "Tell me what's wrong."

"Ma'am, you've got to come down here."

By now I'm screaming and they put an investigator on the line. "Mrs. Whidden, one of your children is missing."

My knees buckled. *Dear, God, help me.*

I don't recall the hour's ride to Dahlonega in a friend's car. Unanswered questions pounded inside my head. *Which child? What happened? A kidnapping? What?!*

I bolted out of the car smack into a bevy of media people with cameras and microphones in hand.

The Sheriff rushed out and escorted me into his office. "Where are my babies? I want to see my babies!" I was becoming hysterical.

Finally I heard him say, "Matthew and Rachel are back there in an office, playing with a computer and eating cookies. But your youngest—the two-year-old—is missing."

"Naomi!? Naomi is missing? What are you saying? Someone took my baby?!" By now, I was totally out of control.

"Your husband said she wandered off while they were hiking. She's lost in the forest."

"Lost? Naomi is lost in the forest?! My baby is out there all alone in those mountains?! It's cold out there. And dark. And raining. And there are wild animals! We've got to find her! Take me there!!"

"We have crews out there searching, Mrs. Whidden. It will be best if you stay here."

"Where is my husband? Where is Duane? Is he out there searching? I want to see Duane!" I needed Duane, desperately. I needed his steadying strength.

"Mr. Whidden is here, but you can't see him right now. We're questioning him, trying to find out what happened."

By nine o'clock, the officers surrendered to my frenzied pleas and drove me out through rugged terrain to the Chattahoochee National Forest.

We passed a roadblock. Then came to a stop where an old logging trail snaked precariously around the side of a mountain. "This is where Mr. Whidden parked his car this morning," the officer told me. "He said the children stopped to play in a clearing about a mile and a half down this trail. He took his eyes off them for a minute. And little Naomi—disappeared."

"I'm going in there," I said, lunging out of the car, toward the steep path. "She'll know my voice and answer me."

"We can't let you do that," a firm hand grasped my shoulder. "You need to stay here for when we bring her out."

I resisted, but without success. All the while, I was calling out across the black forest, "Naomi—Naomi— Mommy's here, Baby. Come to Mommy." My voice was devoured by the vast darkness.

Far away, across the valley, I saw a long line of lights moving slowly through the trees. *The searchers!* "Dear God, please help them find my baby."

Beautiful little Naomi, just turned two. Naomi, with the precious pixie smile and big brown eyes, her light-brown hair tied with a bright ribbon on top of her sweet head. "Please, God, send your angels to look after Naomi."

In the patrol car, I could hear communication between the staging area and searchers in the woods. The radio's every crackle made me hold my breath. At one point an Army helicopter was brought in, giving me hope. Its heat sensors located two coon hunters and a deer. But no little girl.

Then search dogs arrived. In teams of two, they were led down the logging trail, not making a sound. "The dogs will find her if anything can," someone stated. But they didn't.

I shivered in the night air. Temperatures dipped down to 40 degrees. "Naomi—" *Please, God, if they don't find her right away, put her into a deep sleep so she won't feel anything. So she won't feel fear, or cold, or pain. And especially, dear Lord, so she won't feel Mommy and Daddy abandoned her.* It just about killed me to think she might feel we didn't love her.

About midnight, two friends from home were allowed into the forest with me. They put their arms around me and prayed. Duane was brought out to the site at three in the morning. We held each other and cried.

Soon after, the Sheriff drove us home to get Naomi's bed linens so the dogs could pick up her scent. There, in the baby crib, her little brown teddy bear waited. I couldn't watch as the men donned rubber gloves, removed her sheets and pillowcase, and placed them in a plastic bag.

With the coming of daylight, I just *knew* they would find Naomi. But as the hours ticked by and steady rain cast a dreary pall, I experienced an indescribable mental agony. Eventually, my anguished prayers began to include: *Lord, I don't need to know the why of this. And whether I like the result or not, help me to accept it. But, Lord, most of all, I pray you will give Naomi peace in her little heart.*

Meanwhile, among God's angels in heaven, there must have been a great flutter of wings when the prayers came in: "Little Naomi is lost in the forest." And now—Saturday morning—the Master Plan begins to unfold …

9:00 A.M. Kip Clayton, a guard with the Lee Arrendale Correctional Institute, gets a call. His volunteer unit, Habersham County HIGH ANGLE RESCUE TEAM, is needed to search for a two-year-old girl in the Chattahoochee National

Forest. "Oh, dear God. That's the age of my own little girl."
He hurriedly gathers his gear.

10:00 A.M. Al Stowers*—a physician with an Atlanta
hospital—is hiking in the Amicalola Falls area, twenty-five
miles away. "Looking for some of life's answers," he says.
He switches on his pocketsize radio and hears, "Little Naomi
Whidden is still lost in the forest." Dr. Stowers just "happens"
to specialize in Trauma and Pediatric medicine. Besides that, he
has just returned from Alaska where he received special training
in hypothermia. He knows Naomi's time is fast running out.
"I've got to help find her." He hurries to his vehicle.

1:50 P.M. Back at the search area, more than 200 professionals
and volunteers are combing the forest. Those in charge tell them
to make one more sweep. Hope is fast running out and they are
being forced to abandon the effort.

Making that final sweep, Kip Clayton leads his search team
to the outer limit of their assigned area. Reluctantly, he turns
to begin his sweep back. But wait. "Something" tells him to go
an additional 250 yards. He does. Then: "I turn and take two
steps. She is lying five feet in front of me." Shocked, he yells to
his teammates, "I see her!"

Kip fears she is dead. She is lying so still. Face down in
wet leaves and mud, "just as close up against a log as she could
get." Then a tiny whimper—almost like a sigh—comes from
the little soaked body. "She's alive!" he shouts into the radio,
"She's alive!" Awed, Kip knows in his heart, *God led me right
to her.*

1:50 P.M. Just seconds earlier, Dr. Stowers arrives at the
staging area. He is turned away as "not needed." He scribbles
his car phone number down anyway and leaves it. He has the
motor running, his car in gear, when someone runs toward him,
"Don't leave. We've found her! She's alive!" He reaches the

172

ambulance just in time to see it is a "Load and go" situation. "I'm right behind you" he calls out to the driver as they both speed off toward the local hospital.

1:50 P.M. Mirna Whidden continues her story: In the patrol car, Duane and I hear Kip's shouts over the radio—"She's alive! She's alive!" Relief and gratitude fill my being. "Oh, Duane. She's alive."

"They're rushing her to an ambulance," an excited officer tells us. "We'll meet them at St. Joseph!"

We beat them there. As they hurry into ER, I can only call out to the little form within the huge cocoon of blankets, "Naomi, baby. Mommy and Daddy are here. We love you!"

Naomi is pronounced critical. She is unconscious, swollen, blue. Her temperature registers 74 degrees; her heart rate just 70 beats per minute. "I doubt if she could have survived out there another two hours," Dr. Stowers tells us. We pray.

Ordering warmed intravenous fluid for Naomi, Dr. Stowers and the local medical team work feverishly to stabilize her enough for transport to Egleston Children's Hospital in Atlanta for more intensive care. Dr. Stowers asks the Director of Nurses "Can you get me a Pediatric Nurse to travel with us?" And Gail Blankenship, a highly-skilled nurse who works p.r.n. (as needed) locally, but with regular week-end duty at Scottish-Rite Children's Hospital in Atlanta, just "happens" not to have left yet for work. Upon calling Atlanta and explaining the emergency, a co-worker "is led" to work an extra shift so Gail can help Naomi.

An hour later, in the ambulance transporting Naomi to Egleston, space is tight as they tuck us in around her: Sherrie, the Respiratory Specialist sits at Naomi's head, operating the breathing bag; an EMT at her left checks all the equipment; the pediatric nurse, Gail is to her right, keeping the IV tubes functioning; Dr. Stowers, at her feet, watches the heart monitor.

They position me so I can talk to her and pat her little head, barely visible above the heated-air blanket.

Naomi's temperature is still precariously low. She continues to be unresponsive. But wait! Do I detect a movement in her fingers? I gently lay my index finger in her hand and weakly, very weakly, her little fingers close around it.

Mid-way to Atlanta, Naomi's eyes flutter. "Mama."

We all gasp. I continue to gently stroke her forehead, whispering, "Naomi, baby. Mommy's here."

Then a faintly audible, "Mama, song."

I know what she wants. I start singing softly, "Jesus loves me this I know, for the Bible tells me so." Sherrie sings, too. And then, unbelievably, little Naomi—through swollen and chapped lips—tries to join in. I look around at the circle of amazed expressions. Dr. Stowers makes no effort to hide the huge tears spilling down his face. Nor do we. *Dear Jesus who loves Naomi, thank you, thank you, thank you!*

On arrival at Egleston, Naomi's condition still was listed as critical. She was not yet fully conscious—indeed slept through most of Sunday. But on Monday, she woke up—her normal self! As her Dad laughingly describes it, "she perked right up and trashed the room." Later that day, she *walked* to the car. Our little family came home—together.

I can never say thank-you enough to all those who took time from their busy lives to rescue little Naomi. They have my undying gratitude and my prayers that they will be blessed beyond measure.

In the future, if ever I wonder whether or not God hears and answers prayers, I'll remember this experience. For only God and His ministering angels could have orchestrated such a miraculous set of circumstances. Yes, He hears. And answers.

TO GOD BE THE GLORY!

---

* NOTE: Name of the doctor was changed to protect his privacy.

One Wondrous Night in Fredericktown

As written for: Fred Breed

"Call unto me, and I will answer thee, and show thee great and mighty things, which thou knowest not."
Jeremiah 33:3, KJV

A memorable miracle.

One wintry December, members of our church planned a Christmas party for a small mission we sponsored in a poorer section of town. The date was set and word went out inviting all to come for dinner.

New on the job as their just-out-of-seminary pastor, I, along with my wife Sarah Kathryne, eagerly pitched in to help. The ladies cooked all afternoon for the forty or so people expected to attend. The aroma of turkey, green beans, and yams filled the little fellowship building behind the church. One of my jobs was to stack plates at the end of the table and everyone was to come by and be served, cafeteria style.

But when serving time came, the line of people stretched all the way out the door and down the sidewalk. There were close to two hundred persons waiting to eat!

We all looked at each other, asking, "What are we going to do? We don't have enough food for all these people!"

Knowing we couldn't turn *anyone* away and sounding much more confident than I felt, I led the customary prayer, asking God to bless the food. Then, silently, I added a fervent, *Lord, help us!* I'll admit, though, I had no idea how He might do that.

The serving line began moving and we started dipping into the pots. And the more we served, the more food appeared in those pots. We kept dipping. And we kept serving. Until all two hundred people were fed. Then we packaged up leftovers for them to carry home!

That miracle happened in 1956. During all these years of serving as a minister, I've seen the Lord do many wondrous works. But never have I been as awed at His divine intervention as on that wintry night at the First Baptist Church in Fredericktown, Missouri. That night when Jesus reenacted one of His New Testament miracles—and fed *our* multitude with the equivalent of two fishes and five loaves of bread.[1]

And reminded us in a new and marvelous way that His birthday truly *is* one to be celebrated.

---

1   Luke 9:16-17, KJV

The Night an Angel Sang

Not believe in miracles?
I'd sooner not believe in rainbows,
and I don't understand them either.
But I've seen them. They are real.
And so it is with miracles.
—Gloria Cassity Stargel
Heaven Came Down

A young Marine wife, in hospital feeling scared and alone, is comforted late at night by a mysterious woman's voice—singing.

At El Toro Marine Corps Air Station in Southern California where my husband Joe was stationed, the clinic physician peered with a lighted instrument into my right eye. "Hmm'm'm'm ..." he murmured to himself.

"What do you see?" I questioned, anxious to learn the cause of my suddenly blurred vision.

"I'm ... not ... sure," he said, maneuvering his head for a different view.

"Is something wrong with my pregnancy?" I blurted out, near panic. *Please, God, this is our first baby. Don't let anything go wrong.*

"Mrs. Stargel," the young doctor's brow creased, "your vision has deteriorated from 20/20 to 20/70. You need a specialist. I'm sending you to Camp Pendleton Naval Hospital."

Then he added, gently, "You'll need to go prepared to stay." *No, please, no. This can't be happening. Joe's getting discharged next week and we're going home!*

I was *so* homesick! It was my first year away from the rest of the family in Georgia, and we hadn't told them about our baby due in four months. We wanted to surprise everyone! But now ...

That afternoon, Joe and I drove down the Pacific Coast Highway toward San Diego and Camp Pendleton. Ordinarily, we enjoyed the spectacular scenery along Route 101—crashing waves on one side of the road, rolling hills on the other, wild flowers everywhere. But on this day, we saw none of the beauty—concern for my health and that of our baby nearly blocked out the sun.

I checked into the military hospital, a sprawling one-story structure painted inside and out in battleship gray. The antiseptic smell assaulted my senses and threatened to reactivate my morning sickness. They assigned me to a ward with seven other women patients—eight beds lined up "at attention," each with its own metal nightstand in which the washcloth and bedpan, even my toothbrush, had its precise location. Reluctantly, I changed from my first maternity dress—a hunter green two-piece—into gray-blue cotton pajamas bearing the stamp "U.S. Navy."

For the next eleven days doctors examined and x-rayed me, head to toe, trying to locate the area of infection that caused inflammation of the choroid layer of my eye. Inflammation which threatened blindness.

Meantime, they prescribed cortisone to be administered intravenously. My veins proved "uncooperative". Every day, the nurses probed with needles—again and again—while I cringed in pain.

178

Saturday night came. Joe had the weekend duty at El Toro, fifty miles away. My closest neighbors in the ward had left. I hadn't even seen the IV team that day. Never had I felt so forlorn—so forsaken. As the outside darkness smothered the hospital windows, loneliness—loneliness as thick as fog from the nearby ocean—engulfed me.

Sometime after the ten o'clock "lights out," I heard the shuffling of padded feet and the rhythmic tinkle of metal-tubing closures hitting against a bottle of liquid. The sounds stopped by my bed. With lowered voices, working by flashlights so as not to waken the patients on the far end of the ward, the IV team started the vein-search in my bruised arms. I bit my lip.

"I'm sorry, Mrs. Stargel," one of the nurses said. "I wish we didn't have to do this to you, especially at this time of night. Several emergencies kept us from getting to you sooner."

I turned away and clenched my teeth, waiting for the next puncture. *Please!* Finally, sounding relieved for both of us, she said "This one's going to work." As she taped the offending needle onto the back of my wrist, she added, "I'm afraid, though, you won't get much sleep tonight."

Handing me a flashlight, she motioned to the bottle of liquid swinging above my head. "Remember to check from time to time the number of drops per minute. We don't want the medication to enter the body too quickly—nor too slowly." With that bit of instruction, she retreated with the others.

I was alone again. With my free hand I hugged the sheet up under my chin, fighting an onrush of unspeakable sadness. Doubts piled on top of one another. *What if we can't go home next week? What if I lose my eyesight? And our baby! What are all these X-rays and chemicals doing to our baby?*

I wanted, *needed* to pray, but was afraid to try. Would God remember me? After all, I had neglected *Him* this entire year. It was as if I had left God on the East Coast, too—rarely praying, let alone attending church services.

My arm throbbed. I reached for the flashlight, directed its beam on the bottle of medication, and counted the dripping clear liquid: *one, two, three, four ...*

I switched off the light and stared up into the black void. Sinking into a pit of despair, my very soul cried out to God. "Lord, please help me. I know I don't deserve it, God, but please help me."

Soon after—around midnight it was—I couldn't believe what I was hearing! From somewhere—from out in the shadowy hallway—came the hauntingly beautiful sound of a young woman's voice—singing. *Singing!* Singing that lovely Rodgers and Hammerstein song "You'll Never Walk Alone"!

I dared not breathe—afraid the moment would vanish. *I must be dreaming. Who would be singing at this time of night?*

But yes. She was singing all right. In a voice as clear, as soul lifting, as the music of a carillon's steepled bells echoing across a soft green meadow ...

The lyrics were not spiritual, as such. Yet as I listened, amazed, heaven-sent words of hope—and comfort—and courage—winged their way into the ward. And into my waiting heart.

Instantly I was wrapped in a blanket of love—God's love.

As I rested in that newfound refuge, tears I had fought back all evening spilled over, ran down the sides of my face, and puddled in my ears.

When the last note of the celestial song dissolved into memories, I lay there—awed—my fear replaced by perfect peace, my loneliness by the reassurance of a Holy Presence. For Jesus was there.

Finally, I took one more count of the IV drops, laid the flashlight beside my pillow, and fell sound asleep.

The identity of the singer remains a mystery. Did God send an angel to sing for me that night? I believe He did. I believe He wanted to remind me of His promise, "Never will I leave you; never will I forsake you" (Hebrews 13:5b, NIV).

Five days after the angel sang, the hospital dismissed me and the Marine Corps dismissed Joe. We came home.

In time, my vision returned to normal. Scarred, but normal. And our baby—a handsome, healthy son—is all grown up now.

As to "You'll Never Walk Alone", in the years since the angel sang, that song has become a classic, inspiring countless others—in one way or another.

Doctors never found the cause for my eye inflammation. Specialists today, though, tell me the scars indicate I suffered the very serious parasitic infection: toxoplasmosis. An infection which often causes blindness.

This morning—decades later—I'm visiting my oph-thalmologist for a periodic check-up. Dr. Bradley adjusts his instruments and peers deep into the inner layers of my eyes. As he examines the evidence of my California trauma, he murmurs to himself, "Hum'm'm'm ...

And in less time than it takes to tell it, my mind replays the events of that night the angel sang. Once again, I silently ponder: *Was she a supernatural being? Or a human being— an Angel in White?* I may never know. But that's all right. God uses both to send us messages.

Pushing back his chair, now, Dr. Bradley gives me a serious look. "Gloria," he says, "I cannot tell you how *near* you were to losing your eyesight." He indicates with his thumb and fore-finger a minuscule unit of measurement: "That's how close you came to being blinded in that eye."

Dr. Bradley starts to leave the room. At the door he hesitates, then turns back towards me. "Gloria," he says, shaking his head in astonishment, "*Somebody* was looking out for you."

"Yes, I know."

Then—I smile. "He still is."

Hot Wires!

"Nothing is so high and above all danger
That is not below and in the power of God."
Ovid *Tristia, IV, 8, 47*

A young truck driver narrowly escapes death, and sees God's hand at work.

Just as he always did when working, for the trip that night, Darrell Colter wore blue jeans, western cut boots, and a leather belt sporting his prized silver cowboy buckle. It didn't matter that he was delivering a load of alfalfa meal from Alabama to North Carolina, because Darrell grew up riding horses and still fancied himself a cowhand. Although now-a-days, instead of riding a horse he's more apt to be driving an eighteen-wheeler, and instead of an open range, he's traveling the open road.

Darrell kissed his wife, Christina, goodbye, said a quick prayer for safety, then hit the trail. He looked forward to a night of good gospel music from the radio. Not that he'd always been all that religious. He'd been a Christian since he was just a little fella, but as a teenager he got away from the Lord.

Until about four years ago, that is. That's when Darrell decided to clean up his life. Started going to church, driving the van to pick up youngsters for Sunday School ... Now he was even scheduled to be ordained a deacon the following Sunday. That night on the road he kept thinking, *If I had the courage, I could help others to know Jesus, maybe share with them the joy to be found in a close walk with the Lord.*

Darrell reached his destination before daybreak, and wrestled his rig to a groaning stop on a packed-dirt parking lot. The company appeared to be a family-style industry serving the farmers in the region. The typical wood-floor porch ran across the front of the building providing a ramp for small trucks to back up and load their purchases of feed, fertilizer, and farm equipment. All was quiet at that hour though, so he crawled up onto the bunk in his cab, and fell asleep.

About mid-morning, he heard knocking on his door. The foreman of the company broke the news. "Colter, there's been a mix-up" he said, all the while eyeing Darrell's loaded-with-alfalfa-meal hopper trailer, a gigantic metal funnel on wheels. "The broker sent the wrong kind of truck," the foreman explained. "We don't have the pit required to unload from your trailer."

Glancing over the foreman's shoulder, Darrell saw men scratching their heads, trying to figure out what to do with his load of alfalfa meal. "We could send him about twenty miles up the road to a place with a pit," one ventured, "then haul the meal back to here by dump trucks ..."

Darrell decided that while they were figuring, he'd just finish out his nap. For some reason he did something he didn't normally do: he took off his belt with the huge metal buckle.

The next thing he knew a commotion outside got Darrell's attention and he stumbled down from the cab, not even bothering to put on his belt. Men were laying a giant tarp down on the ground; others were pulling a portable auger out from a building. *I've never seen anybody try this before,* he thought to himself, as he cranked up his diesel and worked the truck up over the tarp and auger.

The auger was able to pull the meal from the bottom of the trailer, but without the pull of gravity that they get from a pit, the process was painfully slow. Trying to help things along, Darrell climbed the ladder to the top of the trailer—about ten feet off the ground—and stood on the side with one foot on the metal ledge, the other on the folded-back vinyl tarp that had covered the meal. From there, he poked with a wooden broom handle at the dark green alfalfa meal, keeping it moving toward the caved-in hole which had formed in the center. The stirred-up meal gave off a pleasant, musty smell like fresh-cut hay in the barn back home.

One of the guys on the ground noticed the short pole didn't reach far, and handed Darrell a long metal pole. It worked better. Trouble was, Darrell hadn't noticed the heavy-duty power lines overhead. Within seconds, the pole he held in his hands hit those lines and 13,200 volts of electricity charged through him!

Darrell's body began flopping uncontrollably. As he reeled outward, he saw the ground coming up to meet him. Then, almost as if someone caught him and gave a shove in the opposite direction, he fell toward the truck. Something knocked the pole from his hands, and after his back slammed against the side of the trailer, he tumbled—shoulder first—into the soft alfalfa meal.

Although dazed, Darrell remained conscious, and it all happened so fast, it was as if he had by-passed the moment of pain.

The power-jolt cut off electricity to the mill. Guys rushed out to see what had caused the electrical outage and swung into action when they realized Darrell had nearly been electrocuted.

Two of them clambered over into the meal with him just as he cringed at the extreme heat under his rings. "Get my rings off, quick," he begged. Then his feet felt red-hot! "My boots, my boots, get 'em off, get'em off!"

Around the wheels of the truck, the ground looked as if someone had sprayed black paint. "Talk about heat!" bystanders proclaimed, shaking their heads, "Melted the rubber right off the tires."

A rescue squad arrived, laced Darrell into a wire mesh body-basket and manually hoisted his 6 ft. 1 in, 195 lbs. out of the trailer and into an ambulance.

Medical staff in the emergency room seemed amazed that he was alive. They cautioned that his life still was in danger. They expected his body to swell, all his bodily functions to fail. "We'll know something in 48 hours," the doctor said.

As soon as they allowed, Darrell telephoned his mother back in Georgia. "I need you to go over to the house," he told her. "I want you to be with Christina when she gets the news."

By eight o'clock that evening, Darrell lay strapped to a gurney aboard a medi-vac helicopter bound for the burn unit of Duke University Hospital over in Durham.

His family, after quickly starting up some prayer chains, drove the 340 miles as fast as they dared so they could be by his side. They prepared for the worst—but prayed for the best.

God blessed them with the best. After two days, the doctor showed Darrell how to treat his wounds—burns on one finger, on the palm of his hand that held the pole, and on his foot that was standing on the metal edge. No swelling, no internal damage. He then dismissed Darrell with orders to take at least a week off from work. "You're a very lucky young man," the doctor said. Darrell knew better. It was God's divine protection. And his life would be forever changed.

Darrell's brother Jody offered to drive the truck back to Georgia, and Darrell rode home with his parents. On the way, it was as if God spoke to him. "Darrell," He said, "I want you to get prepared so you will have the confidence to tell others about me." Darrell searched his memory for that scripture about being prepared with the gospel, about putting on the whole armor, something about the belt of truth. *Belt. My silver belt buckle! Where is it?*

"My buckle," Darrell said to the family. "I left my buckle in the truck."

His mother picked right up on that. "You weren't wearing your buckle when you were hit?" she exclaimed. "Do you suppose that helped protect your internal organs?"

"I hadn't thought of that," he said, shaking his head in wonderment. "Considering the heat that came through my rings, I shudder to think what it might have done if I'd been wearing the buckle." It was a moment of awe. He *always* wore that buckle.

Once home, Darrell wasted no time in searching the Bible for that scripture about God's armor. He found it in Ephesians 6:10-20; and it was powerful, starting with, "Finally, be strong in the Lord and in His mighty power." It tells us: "Stand firm with the belt of truth buckled around your waist" and "take up the shield of faith, with which you can extinguish all the flaming arrows of the evil one." Darrell bowed his head. *Thank you, Lord, for extinguishing the flaming arrows of that electric charge this week. Thank you.*

Now, Darrell is learning to take up the shield of faith daily by studying God's Word. And when he fastens his silver cowboy buckle, he is reminded to put on his spiritual armor as well. So prepared, he has the courage to share his story with others. He explains to them we all need *internal* armor—*spiritual* armor. The kind that only God can provide. The kind that will see us through the rough places of life.

Darrell is praying that God will continue to give him the boldness to speak up for Him, to tell others about His great love for each of us.

He's already started. For the words Darrell painted on the cab of his new truck invite many questions, and he is ready with the answers. In large red letters the message proclaims: ONLY BY THE GRACE OF GOD.

Out Too Far

As written for: Polly Ismond

*"Praise is awaiting you, O God ... You who still the
noise of the seas, The noise of their waves, And the
tumult of the peoples."*
Psalm 65:1,7a, NKJV

A lapse in good judgment nearly proves fatal for this swimmer.

That warm June afternoon was bright with sunshine and
Lake Michigan was but a short walk away. "Perfect for a
swim before supper," I told myself, quickly gathering my swim
cap, goggles and towel.

Stepping outside the dorm, I paused, admiring tree-
shaded Leelanua School nestled just behind the sand dunes.
*What a beautiful setting for our two-week Elderhostel—great
opportunities for "Close Up Nature Photography".*

No one else was stirring about as I walked the few yards
through the path, over the Crystal River Bridge, to the broad
sand beach. There, I took a few moments more to savor the
scene of gleaming water reaching to the horizon. "Ah, yes!" I
exclaimed inwardly. "This is my kind of day!" Out this morning

at 5:30, shooting photos of a magnificent sunrise. Back to the school for developing and mounting slides. Now about to take an invigorating swim.

Even so, in a corner of my consciousness, a heavy cloud hovered ever near—the fear of completely losing my failing eyesight. Extreme glaucoma was fast taking its toll. I'd already had to make wrenching concessions: giving up driving, reading, the ability to catch the pattern of ripples in a stream . . . *What next?* I worried. *Photography? My outside work and play?*

An active person all my sixty-plus years, I've stayed committed to daily exercise. How would I cope if I couldn't tend our Christmas tree farm, or go canoeing, or cross-country skiing . . . ?

Or worst of all, lose the ability to take care of my basic needs? I've always prided myself on being independent. That trait proved valuable eighteen years earlier when my husband died suddenly leaving me to operate the farm.

Now, with my vision deteriorating, I felt I was being forced into a black tunnel with no exit into the light. I've wanted to ask, "God, have you forgotten me?"

As I stood on the shore of Lake Michigan, that fear surfaced again, "Even though I'm looking through a haze now, what if I can no longer see breath-taking sights like this *at all*?" Unbidden tears appeared.

"Enough of that!" I told myself. "You have *today*. Be grateful you can still see well enough to *swim*."

Not a soul was in sight but that didn't concern me. I am an experienced swimmer with an earned Red Cross Water Safety Instructor badge; years earlier had even belonged to a formation aquatics club. Yet I was about to break a rule I had taught many times at summer camps and at colleges: "Never swim alone."

But, I always swim in waist-deep water, I reasoned. *I'll just swim along the shore until I'm tired. Then I'll walk back.*

Leaving my towel, swim shoes and glasses in a bag on the beach, I put on swim cap and goggles as I strode down to the

188

water's edge. *Windy today*, I observed. *Quite strong from the southwest and making lots of waves.* Taking that into account, I figured I could breathe on my normal right side without a problem.

Wading in, I noticed that even with the waves kicking up, the lake was clear as glass. *Looks inviting* I took a deep breath and plunged into stinging-cold water. "Not so bad," I told myself after a few minutes of vigorous stroking.

My poor eyesight was even worse without my glasses and with the added blur of goggles. All the time, though, I managed to see the sand bottom of the lake beneath me which I gauged to be a safety guide.

The rough water soon turned the hoped-for pleasant swim into a major battle. Swimming on my back was out because of the whipping waves, so I alternated a breaststroke with a crawl. I fought it a long while—until I was completely spent. Chilled and weary, I didn't think I could take another stroke. "That's it for today," I told myself. Drawing up my knees, I put down my feet to walk into shore. *There's no bottom!!*

A little twinge of panic hit me, but I was still not too worried. That is, not until I tried to get oriented. *Which way to go?! In the distance—are those trees, or not? How did I get this far out?!* I turned to what I hoped was land and began valiantly to swim.

Only now I could not breathe on the right side as the waves were coming from there; so I could only swim a breaststroke. I kept putting my feet down to touch bottom. But it was not there.

What if I'm swimming in the wrong direction? "Lord," I cried out, frantically treading water, "which way is land?"

An inner voice said, "Think, Polly, think! Which way is the wind blowing?" *From southwest. The wind is coming from southwest. I must be going pretty much in the right direction.*

Summoning every ounce of reserve strength, I made several more desperate pulls at the unforgiving water.

I had nothing left to give. Panic set in. I tried to turn on my back. The waves splashed over my face. *I'll never recover if I get choked at this point!* My chest hurt. My arms felt like lead. I could scarcely move them. The realization that I was going to drown hit me. "Lord, help me!" I prayed, over and over again. "Lord, please help me!"

My whole life did not pass in front of me. Instead, I thought of the sadness of my children. And strangely, I thought, "I'm going to ruin the week for all these people here." And "I wonder what Jesus will look like?"

I took a deep breath and flopped helplessly on my back, feebly kicking my legs and yelling, "Help!" Even though I knew there was no one to hear.

The water splashed over my face again and I turned back over. My arms refused to move. There was no more thrashing about.

I'm not sure what happened next. Whether from utter exhaustion I had given up and let my feet go down; or whether my subconscious was performing a survival technique where one takes a breath, relaxes and rests with feet hanging down, I don't know.

But a toe touched solid sand!

The rush of adrenalin that provided gave me the strength to take a few more strokes and stagger toward shore—the last part on hands and knees.

I sat down, my face in my hands, and sobbed over and over: "Thank you, God. Thank you, God. Thank you, God." I was shivering, but I remember how wonderful the hot sun felt.

When the flies began to bite, I got up, trudged back to my towel and shoes, and made it back to the dorm. I stood in the hot shower for a long while. Then I drank a glass of hot water from the tap, got dressed and lay down until supper.

That night, I ate with the others, saying nothing to anyone about my ordeal. Then came the slide critique. About half way through the session, a feeling of panic mixed with tears almost overwhelmed me. Thankfully it was pitch dark, so no one noticed.

Afterwards, a gentleman who had recognized my vision difficulties, offered to walk me back to my dorm. At the side of the building we took some steps which had a handrail, and when we were away from the others I asked, "May I share something with you?"

"Of course," he replied. Then held me while I sobbed out my story.

Back home, when I told family and friends about the close call, most chided me for swimming alone. But the response I like best came from one of my sons. He said, "Thanks, Mom, for not giving up."

I've relived the harrowing experience many times. I find it reassuring that the one thing causing the most trouble—the strong wind—was the very thing God used to save my life. Which tells me He can take my vision problems and turn them into something positive, as well. So it is that I face the future with confidence. God is still in charge and He knows my every need.

I thought on these things this morning as I walked out the road to my mailbox and turned up the red flag. The envelope I put inside contained my reservation for next summer's excursion, white-water rafting on the Nantahala River in the rugged North Carolina Mountains.

After that, there's the Appalachian Trail to hike ...

Home for Christmas

As written for: Richard C Stargel

God moves in a mysterious way
His wonders to perform;
He plants His footsteps in the sea
And rides upon the storm.
—William Cowper, Hymn
"Light Shining Out of Darkness"

This little family needed special help to get there this year.

It's 5:00 o'clock in the afternoon on December 27. At the Dallas/Fort Worth Airport, the terminal teems with edgy travelers studying their watches. Our little family of three maneuvers past computer screens filled with notices of cancelled and delayed flights. "That winter storm on the East Coast is causing havoc with air travel *everywhere*," I moan.

The public address system keeps up a steady stream of announcements—in Spanish, then English. Harried agents try to cope with countless questions whose answers keep changing. We reach Gate 8. "Flight #832 to Atlanta is on schedule for a

6:43 departure," I read out loud. "What a relief!" For a few moments, I allow "visions of sugarplums" to dance in my head. Only this time, it's Mom's roasted turkey and cornbread stuffing.

"I hope we make it," my wife, Lisa, says, settling our little nine-month-old Richard to playing with his toys. "I know your parents want to see Richard enjoy his first Christmas."

"Oh, yes," I answer. "Too bad I had to work Christmas day." In my mind, I picture Mom and Dad, waiting to celebrate Christmas until the family could be together, a practice they started while I was on active duty with the Marine Corps. "My mother is like a mama cat with her brood of kittens," I tell Lisa, "fully content only when we are safely gathered close by."

"Why don't you call them and check on the weather in Georgia?" Lisa asks. It's hard to realize that icy conditions are paralyzing everything there, while out here we just rode past mesquite trees with brilliant sunshine glancing off bare limbs.

I dial home and report: "Mom says it's getting worse. Freezing rain and sleet are making driving hazardous. Hartsfield International reports dense fog plus air traffic already backed up due to blizzards in the Northeast."

"On top of the threatening weather," Lisa adds, "it was a bit unnerving to see that television report just before coming out to the airport."

"About the unscheduled landing here this afternoon?" I silently recall the facts: *A Falcon jet flying from Seattle to Atlanta made an unscheduled landing due to problems with its hydraulic system used to steer the craft on the ground.*[1]

"I'd just as soon not be reminded that airplanes have problems just before we fly off into the wild blue yonder." Lisa manages a grin.

---

1   Name of Airline changed.

"The good news is," I reassure her, "All 228 passengers came away unhurt." I send up a hasty, *Lord, please give us a safe trip home.*

As time drags on, Richard gets restless. "Lisa, if you'll stay with the bags, I'll walk him around awhile." The two of us reach Gate 15 where I chance to hear a red-coated Falcon employee speak with a tone of concern into his walkie-talkie: "Flight #832 has been cancelled?"

My ears snap to attention. "Did you say Flight #832 has been cancelled? That's *my* flight!"

"Yes," he replies. "That plane is being held at its departure point. If you want to get to Atlanta tonight, you'd better get on *this* one in a hurry. Air traffic at Hartsfield is so snarled, we have only a fifteen-minute window to get in there."

With that, Richard and I do an about-face and sprint off down the concourse to gather up Lisa and our gear. We hustle back to Gate 15. Flight attendants double as gate attendants. "It's open seating," they say as they rush us aboard. Inside the cavernous aircraft, we—along with a handful of other passengers—take our pick of seats. Within moments, the plane pushes back from the gate.

We're airborne when we hear a flight attendant mention "Seattle." Lisa and I exchange startled looks that say, *Oh, Oh! We're on the 767 that landed at Dallas this afternoon due to mechanical problems.* Of course, common sense tells me the airline would not let the plane fly if it were not ready. Still . . . *Dear Lord, protect us,* I pray.

My concern travels to Georgia. *I'm sure our family has learned about our cancelled flight. They're wondering where we are and why we don't phone.* I picture the house, decorated from top to bottom. And on the coffee table, in its traditional place of honor, is our unique nativity scene—unique because it consists of only two figures. The Bible is opened to the Christmas story in Luke, chapter two, and just in front of the

Bible is a small ceramic figure of the Christ Child. Watching over Him—lovingly, prayerfully—is His mother.

By now, *my* mother is peering out the window for the hundredth time, worrying about the weather. And praying we'll get a flight out and a safe trip home. *Please, Lord . . .*

About 10:00 o'clock, aboard the 767, the "Fasten Seatbelts" lights flash on. The captain announces, "We're making our final approach into Hartsfield." I look out the window. Fog is so thick our landing lights bounce back at us off the mist. A runway is nowhere to be seen. I pray the hydraulic system is in good working order, then listen for the lowering of landing gear. *Thump, Groan, Grind.* Perfectly normal sounds, I tell myself. But I admit that my breath catches as the wheels impact the runway. They hold. Whew! *Thank you, Lord.*

We spill out into the terminal at Hartsfield International and locate a pay phone to call home. "Mom?"

"Where *are* you?" she asks, sounding relieved to hear my voice. "Back at your apartment in Texas?"

"No, Ma'am, we're at the Atlanta airport."

"But you can't be!" Mom exclaims. "We've talked with Falcon Airlines several times. There was not another flight coming in tonight! How in the world did you get here—on a *phantom flight?*"

"You're not going to believe it," I say, somewhat in awe myself. "I'll tell you the whole story when we get home."

We collect our rental car and cautiously head north on I-85 for the 50-mile drive to Gainesville. In his car seat, travel-weary Richard falls sound asleep. Picking our way through thick fog and treacherous black ice on the highway, I hear the radio announcer report road closings and power outages and poor visibility. On the open road, our headlights occasionally pierce the grayness to reveal tall, skinny pine trees bending almost to the ground, their needles coated with ice.

At last, we're almost home and I replay in my mind the events of the past several hours. "You know, Lisa," my voice breaks the silence, "if I hadn't been walking Richard we wouldn't have caught that plane. We'd still be in Texas."

"And Richard would be terribly out-of-sorts by now," she adds.

"Yes. And think how remote the possibility was that when we needed a plane to Atlanta, one was sitting there—completely unplanned—ready to take off. And an almost *private, gigantic* plane, at that!

"Besides," I go on, "our original flight would have been in a much smaller plane, possibly ill-equipped to land under such adverse weather conditions. "*This* one carried all the latest sophisticated equipment!"

"Rick," Lisa responds, "I think we just received a very special Christmas gift—maybe even a miracle!"

"I think you're right."

At 12:45 in the morning, tired but safe, we pull into the driveway. All lights of the house are on—outside and inside. The front door swings open and out rush Mom, Dad, and my brother Randy, while the aroma of holiday spices, baking turkey, and burning logs waft their way to my senses.

In the living room, we become a Christmas-card scene with more hugs and laughter, a roaring fire in the fireplace, bright twinkling lights on the tree, and tinkling bells playing *Silent Night, Holy Night.*

While on the coffee table, the tiny ceramic figure of Mary beams down on her babe in the manger. Yes, it is good to be home! *Thank you, Jesus*, I say silently from my heart. "*And again, thank you.*"

I join the others around the tree, then do an about-face toward the little Nativity Scene. *Oh, and Sir,* I whisper, *Happy Birthday.*

Devastation at Dawn

As written for: Brenda Harvey

[Jesus Christ] *"who has gone into heaven and is at God's right hand—with angels, authorities and powers in submission to Him."*
1Peter 3:22, NIV

Tornado!

Six twenty A.M. Buzzzz! The alarm clock at our bedside jarred me half-awake. I reached over and hit the snooze control. *Ah! Thirty more minutes before starting my day.* In the distance I detected a roll of thunder. But last night's weather forecast had issued no severe-storm warnings, so I drifted back into a peaceful sleep. Beside me, my husband, Danny, never stirred.

Just five months earlier, we had completed the building of our home and moved in. Our sons, Chase, 10, and Tyler, 12, had their own rooms and were feeling quite grown up. Yes, life was good. Curled up under a couple of blankets on that morning of March 20, 1998, I was as oblivious to the outside world as a bear in hibernation.

6:34 A.M. "Mom … Dad …" I became aware of Chase standing in our bedroom door. "I think you need to wake up," he said.

I propped up on one elbow, "What's wrong, Chase?" noticing he was visibly shaken. "You're never up this early."

"Something's not right, Mom. And the lights just went out."

Something's not right, I realized with a start. *The air feels strange.* Just then I heard it! Not a freight-train sound, but that of a monster thunder roll that never let up. And it was getting closer. And closer. There was no doubt. **TORNADO!** Fear catapulted me into action. I shook my husband awake. "Danny! Danny! Hurry!"

"Get to the basement, quick!" Danny shouted as he yanked on a pair of pants. I grabbed a robe and raced behind Chase toward the basement stairs. Passing through the kitchen, I saw something I never want to see again—the walls and doors bulged outward. Through the windows a gray mass swirled wildly, a mass so thick I could not see the porch railings.

About the same moment, our fire alarm shrilled into action. "Fire! Leave house immediately!" The outside horn sounded full blast, competing with the horror of the twister's increasing roar.

Just then a deadly calm settled over everything—a calm like nothing I'd ever experienced. Not a sound could be heard. Except the intermittent signal from our smoke alarm. *Dear God in heaven, help us!*

"Go on down, Chase!" I flew into Tyler's room. His bed was empty. At the head of the stairs, I yelled, "Tyler, are you down there?" I heard a very frightened, "Yes." "Both of you?" "Yes."

"Hurry, Danny, hurry!" I hollered toward the other end of the house knowing now that a killer storm had us in its sights. We were about to take a direct hit. "Danny!" The tornado-created vacuum blocked my voice mere inches from my face.

The house moaned. Starting down the steps, on the third one I hesitated. Never have I been so torn between. *Where is Danny? What to do I need to be with the children. But I can't leave him up here!*

Seconds later, the choice was made for me.

6:35 AM The roar was upon us. Unleashed fury struck full force at two hundred miles an hour, an F4 tornado. Terrified, I gripped the handrail as I shouted "Danny!" But now the sound was swallowed up in ear-splitting sounds, sounds too horrible to believe, as our home literally exploded around me. Glass shattered, wood splintered, metal crumpled, roofing ripped, insulation shredded, rafters fell, fireplace rocks crashed. Unidentified objects became wild missiles. The odor of Sheetrock dust overwhelmed the senses as walls and ceilings were pulverized. The shrieking wind was deafening.

One wall beside me tore away. I was jerked first one way, then another. Shards of glass and bits of concrete block mixed with red mud bombarded me from all sides. Out of the corner of my eye I spotted a huge black thing flying through the air just before it hit me in the head. The force sent me careening down the stairs, my bare toes doubling under. Everything went black for a few seconds. Yet my subconscious kept saying, *the children. You've got to stay alert for the children.*

Suddenly, it was over. Just as quickly as it began. Another eerie quiet descended. Not a sound. No birds. No nothing.

I forced my eyes open. Chase and Tyler were still standing right where they had been, except they were soaking wet. The vacuum had pulled all the water out of the downstairs commode and drenched them with it. "Are you both okay?" "Yes," they answered shakily, about to cry, "but where is Daddy?" *Danny! Oh, Lord, is he dead?* "You boys stay here." I didn't want them to see what I feared I'd find.

The stairs were blocked with debris. I pushed aside boards, being careful of protruding nails, and lifted what appeared to be part of a door. With great effort I made it to the top. I could not believe my eyes. Without warning—in fifteen seconds of utter devastation—our new home was no more. The only thing not demolished was the back wall of our breakfast room, complete with three unbroken windows. On the other side of that room, where the laundry area used to be, perched Danny's blue and white Ford pickup and our black Jimmy, blown in from the garage. Both were totaled.

I called out a tentative, "Danny?"

"Brenda?"

"Danny!" *Could this be true?* "Danny, where are you? Are you hurt?" Just then I saw him crawling out over the truck. I picked my way toward him.

"No, Brenda, don't come this way! Too much glass. And hot wires. Are the boys safe?"

"Yes, downstairs."

"Go back down with them and come out the basement door."

We met in the front yard, ecstatic to be alive and together. Standing there shivering in our bare feet, we were too much in shock to comprehend what we were seeing. Everything we had was gone. We didn't even own a toothbrush. But we had each other and that is what really mattered. *Thank you, God. Thank you.*

When we calmed down a bit I had to know, "Where *were* you, Danny? Why didn't you come down right behind us?"

"You won't believe this," he said. "I stopped to muffle the smoke alarm. I was afraid it would disturb the neighbors."

"Danny, you could have gotten us both killed!"

"Don't I know it. I guess I was still half asleep and not thinking clearly. But when the back door flew off right beside me, I knew I had waited too long. I just fell down, face first, right where I was. Soon a piece of Sheetrock fell on top of me, protecting me somewhat. And now that I see where my truck ended up, I know it protected me as well."

The room where Danny fell flat happened to be the breakfast room, the one with the only wall still intact. He suffered only minor cuts and bruises. My scalp was embedded with concrete-block chips and glass shards, and my hair—encrusted with red mud—stuck straight out. At the hospital, x-rays ruled out a concussion or broken toe.

When I got back from the emergency room, Danny was standing outside the ruins holding a crumpled birdcage. "Oh, no. Chipper!" Our bright yellow parakeet's cage had been by the fireplace in the living room. We abandoned hope of ever seeing him again.

Two days later, Danny and Tyler were cleaning up the rubble when they heard a faint "Chirp." They looked at each other. *You don't think…?* They began moving a pile of fireplace rocks and there, buried under one, lay a cold, hungry, scared but otherwise unhurt Chipper.

The boys' beds were never found, but part of ours landed on top of my sister's house probably a half mile away. Our fully-stocked camper, which had been parked on the right side of the house, ended up in a field on the other side. That is, the metal frame did—stripped bare. We discovered in our basement the object that hit me on the head—the inner drum of our neighbor's washing machine.

Later, when we could discuss things rationally, I asked Chase, "Honey, what woke you that morning? Whatever it was saved our lives."

Chase hesitated a moment. "I didn't know how to tell you," he started. "I can't say for sure what woke me the first time, but I got up and looked out the window, then went back to bed. That's when it happened. Something—or someone—moved a hand across the back of my hair. I knew I was supposed to come wake you." He gave me a look which said, *You're not going to believe this.* "Mom, it was my guardian angel. I didn't see her, but I know it was."

"Oh, yes, Chase, I believe you," as I grabbed him in bear hug, remembering that within scant moments of his leaving his room, that room was obliterated. As was Tyler's room—and ours!

Without warning? It appears that we got an advance warning after all. A warning from Chase's guardian angel.

Skeptics might say static electricity caused Chase's hair to stand on end. I don't worry about that, though. It is enough that in the midst of the storm, God brought us through. And I know now that when future storms rage about me—which they will, of one kind or another—I can continue to rest in His care—safe and secure.

NOTE: This article first appeared in the Mar/Apr 2002 issue of *Christian Reader.*

CHAPTER 6

Jesus, Our Refuge

Resting in His Safe Harbor

*I've anchored my soul
In the haven of rest
I'll sail the wide seas no more;
The tempest may sweep
O'er the wild, stormy deep
In Jesus I'm safe evermore.*

H. L. Gilmore
George D. Moore

"The Haven of Rest"
Baptist Hymnal, © 1956 Convention Press, Nashville, TN

The Peacekeeper

" Where there is peace, God is. "
George Herbert
Jacula Prudentum no.729

His leisure time was far from peaceful.

The day our younger son Rick left home for the Marine Corps was a heart-wrenching one for me. Besides the fact that I just hate goodbyes, this was my "baby" going off to become a fighting man. I couldn't help worrying that military training would destroy Rick's loving, compassionate spirit. *Dear Lord, make him tough, if necessary. But, please, Lord, I* prayed, *keep him tender.* Now who but a mother would make a request like that?

Rick endured the rigors of basic training and Officer Candidate School. Then, after advanced instruction, he was assigned to the Marine Corps Air Station in Cherry Point, NC. There—seeking a little off-duty peace and quiet of his own—he rented a small house out in the country. Always athletic, he looked forward to the solitude of his daily six-mile run along picturesque fields and meadows.

A problem developed, though. It seems that each farm had several large dogs. They didn't take too kindly to this strange intruder racing through their territories. Every day, by the time Rick made it back to his house, he was tripping over a whole pack of yelping dogs, most of them snarling at his heels. It was *not* the tranquil time he had envisioned. Hoping to discourage the attackers, he tried kicking, swinging a stick, yelling. Nothing worked.

One day, Rick phoned home. "Mother," he began, "you know those dogs that have been making my life miserable? Well, I remembered you taught us "kindness always pays." So I decided to give it a try."

"What did you do?" I asked.

"Yesterday as I ran," he said, "when my patience had been pushed to the limit, I just stopped in my tracks, whirled around to face them, stooped down on one knee, and talked to them in my best 'pet-talk' voice. And you know what?" Rick's voice was smiling now. "Those dogs started wagging their tails and kissing me on the face, each trying to get closer than the other."

"What happened today when you ran?" I wanted to know.

"You wouldn't believe the difference," Rick said. "It was *so* peaceful! Passing one farm after the other, the whole crowd fell in and ran as usual. But this time they ran *with* me—not against me. I must have looked like the Pied Piper by the time we got back to my house."

I smiled into the phone, picturing my young, still-sensitive son. For Rick had solved his problem. And God had answered this Mother's prayer.

America, Standing Tall

"Blessed is the nation whose God is the LORD."
Psalm 33:12A, KJV

A volunteer receives an unexpected blessing.

It happened on a cold December night. At *Babyland General®
Hospital* in Cleveland, Georgia, of all places! This birthplace
of the famous *Cabbage Patch* Kids ® was hosting a promotional
event for the U.S. Marine Corps' Annual *Toys for Tots* ®.

Fun activities were in full swing, everywhere a festive
atmosphere. Inside the white frame building, youngsters
watched with eyes wide as uniformed "nurses" in the *cabbage
patch* "delivered" cloth babies.

Outside, where colorful, twinkling, lights adorned every
accessible tree and shrub, exuberant volunteers manned hotdog
stands, popcorn machines, and hot chocolate dispensers, while
excited children awaited the arrival of the High School band
escorting a horse-drawn wagon bearing Santa Claus!

Singing groups gathered on the makeshift stage under a
marquee of bare-limbed oaks, their "Silent Nights" and "Up
on the Housetops" wafting along the winter breezes.

Listening to the Toys for Tots Singers, I stood next to our
area Marine recruiter. The young sergeant was the *picture* of a

proud Marine—shoulders back, chest out. Wearing dress blues, white cover positioned squarely on his head, the sergeant's black shoes were shined so brightly they mirrored the colorful, twinkling lights.

From out of the milling crowd appeared a young man with his daughter—she must have been about five "Pardon me, Sergeant," he said. "May my little girl have a word with you?"

Appearing somewhat taken aback, the Marine nodded "yes."

Whereupon the child, with great dignity, walked around to face him. Drawing herself up to full height, possibly 2½ feet, she fixed her gaze upon the ribbons on his chest, placed her right hand over her heart and, with utmost solemnity, began, "I pledge allegiance to the flag of the United States of America …"

The sergeant quietly shifted position from *At Ease* to *Attention* while, in a clear small voice, the little one recited the Pledge to its conclusion, "one nation, under God, indivisible, with liberty and justice for all."

The Marine's trained-to-be-tough features never flinched. But as a light beam caught his face, I detected something in his eye that wanted to be a tear. I know, because I choked down one myself.

For to that dear child, the young Marine sergeant *was* America. And how fitting. Because, indeed, a Marine—like America itself—is a tough fighter if necessary. But when allowed, each has a considerate, tender heart.

Whether it's gathering toys for needy children at Christmas, or airdropping food to the enemy in the midst of war, Americans much prefer a kinder, gentler role. Yet, they stand ever ready to do whatever is necessary to defend their way of life—their freedom.

At Babyland General that cold December night, I saw America at its finest. In the Marine serving his country. In the little girl showing respect. In everyday people giving their time and resources, wanting nothing more than for children everywhere to have a happy Christmas.

America—standing tall.

My America.

One nation, under God.

⚓

My Day as a TV Star

"If Shakespeare should come into this room,
We would all rise;
But if Jesus Christ should come in,
We would all kneel."
Charles Lamb
12,000 Religious Quotations

An author learns that fame is relative.

It is Tuesday noon when the telephone rings. I am home, scrubbing the bathroom. To my "hello" a pleasant female voice responds, "Gloria Stargel, please."

Recognizing an out-of-Georgia accent on the other end of the line, I try shifting into a more professional voice. "This is she," I answer.

The out-of-Georgia voice says, "This is Jean Williams in Tulsa, Oklahoma. I'm calling for the Richard Roberts Show."

Now I need to explain at the outset, we're talking big time here. Richard Roberts is the son of world-renowned evangelist Oral Roberts. The Richard Roberts Show is telecast daily from a studio on the campus of Oral Roberts University in Tulsa. It is seen via satellite by literally millions of people throughout the world.

So when the telephone call comes, I am a mite incredulous. Into the phone, though, I try to sound nonchalant, "Yes?"

"Mrs. Stargel, can you come to Tulsa and appear on our Thursday morning show?"

I respond, "Let me check my calendar and get back with you." Whereupon, I immediately phone my beautician, "Can you do my hair right away?" I mean, first things first.

Two days later, I am in Tulsa, ready for my big television appearance.

I might explain that this is operating outside my comfort zone—flying alone, appearing on television … yet I do have my book *The Healing* to promote, and to do that I will go anywhere.

At the studio on Thursday morning, Jean ushers me behind the set into a flurry of activity. There's a certain air of expectancy before a television show goes on the air, probably akin to that of a Broadway production just before the curtain rises.

I shake hands with Richard Roberts, his co-host Billy Joe Dougherty, TV production head Harry Salem, and guest coordinator Jeff Geuder.

Then Jean asks, "Would you like to go in and watch the first show? It'll help you get the feel of things."

"I'd love it" I tell her, pretending I do this kind of thing every day. She parts the heavily-insulated gray curtains and we parade before the live audience assembled in the studio, all the while dodging camera dollies, and tip-toeing around heavy cables—the umbilical cords of the production.

Suddenly, the music starts, and everyone springs to life. The announcer proclaims, "The Oral Roberts Ministries present Richard Roberts!" And Richard Roberts—a perfect example of "tall, dark, and handsome"—strides onto the set, microphone in hand, singing the show's lively theme song, "Turn It Around" (Message: "God can turn your life around.")

While the ORU Singers, an effervescent assemblage of talented young Oral Roberts University students, render another number, Richard walks over to the side of the studio, and sits on the couch in the "living 'room" set. He is joined by his wife, Lindsay, and co-host Billy Joe.

Also in the studio, on an upper level just behind all this action, I can see the abundant Life Prayer Group—men and women volunteers manning a bank of telephones, receiving prayer requests and testimonies of answered prayers.

Midway through the hour-long show, Jean leans over and whispers, "Let's go check with 'makeup' to see if you're OK." I consider requesting a major overhaul. Instead, I quietly follow her out through a side curtain.

We return to the studio just as the first show finishes. Richard declares a 15-minute break, and then with all the spirit and enthusiasm as before, they begin the taped show.

I again take my place in the audience, except this time I am told to sit on the front row. Close to the living-room set.

About 45 minutes into the program while the cameras are on the singers, Richard jumps to his feet, turns toward me, and crooks his finger, motioning me to join them.

Billy Joe stands and says "hello again;" Richard introduces me to Lindsay and says, "Your microphone is by the couch cushion." A young man wearing earphones steps up to help me adjust my mike. The lights brighten and all cameras converge on our corner. We are ON.

From here on my memory blurs. I will learn how well the interview went at the same time you do—when we view the telecast.

But time passes swiftly, the camera lights cut off, and Richard thanks me for coming. He adds, "I have a copy of your book. I want you to have a copy of mine."

With that, he sits back down and writes a note to "Joe and Gloria" in the front of his new book *He's The God of a Second Chance.*

We say goodbye with hugs all around.

Soon, Jean takes me back under her wing and we climb upstairs to meet some more people, one of whom is Cheryl Prewitt, Miss America of 1980. Cheryl, a gorgeous, effervescent brunette, regularly sings on the show. Upon learning I am from Gainesville where we have mutual friends, she greets me with more hugs. (Born-again Christians do a lot of hugging.)

After a fine lunch, Jean delivers me to the airport for my flight home.

Thus ended my day as the TV star—a memorable twenty-four hours. But alas, fame is fleeting. Now I'm back to my housewifely chores and the quiet life of a writer.

But who knows? One of these days the phone might ring again. Maybe I'll keep my luggage handy, just in case.

A Soul-Lifting Place

— Gloria Cassity Stargel

"And the LORD, whom ye seek,
shall suddenly come to His temple.
Malachi 3:1b, KJV

The little chapel grew right out of the ground.
Its rock walls and slate roof nestled at the base
of a gentle slope, reached by a flagstone walkway
curving through graceful oaks and stately pines.
At its side flowed a gentle stream, its water gliding
over smooth stones, creating a soothing waterfall.
It faced a small, quiet lake—a lake as still as a whisper.
I think I've never seen a more tranquil, soul-lifting place.
I felt the love and prayers of uncounted others who had
knelt there.
I felt the realness of God. Soon I would be back in the
hurrying
and worrying of the world, but I knew
that I would not forget this glimpse of God's
presence. Yet, if I keep my awareness attuned to
God, He will show me other glimpses of His
presence—
whether in a serene setting,
a spectacular sunset,
or a special smile.

An Angel's First Christmas

"This is Christmas: not the tinsel, not the giving and receiving, not even the carols, but the humble heart that receives anew the wondrous gift, the Christ."
—Frank McKibben,
12,000 Religious Quotations

Their live nativity scene comes to life for this "angel."

My tinsel-edged angel wings in place, I waited with the rest of the cast for the shift change of our live Nativity scene.

Area residents looked forward each Christmas to our reenactment of that holy night, staged by the young people and adults of our church. On the front lawn—complete with real animals and swathed in floodlights—our Nativity scene was a sight to behold.

A sense of anticipation filled the education-building-turned-dressing room that evening. Volunteers made last-minute adjustments to the humble robes of shepherds, the gold-trimmed garments of wise men, the soft folds of Mary's gown. The director's head appeared in the doorway, "Time to go."

Out we scurried into a blustery, below-freezing December night. A gust of wind whipped my angel wings until I wondered

215

if I might take to the skies like the Christmas angels of old. It seemed the only thing anchoring me to the ground was the heavy clothing under my white robe.

Whispering in total darkness, we stumbled in the direction of the stable, a temporary structure of rough slabs. Pine boughs on either side represented trees.

One angel climbed up to sit on top of the stable. Around at the entrance, a shepherd pulled and pushed a reluctant donkey into the stall while the rest of us took our places.

All at once, brilliant lights switched on. There we stood, transfixed in time, mirroring to the world a glorious scene—the newborn baby Jesus.

The star of Bethlehem, suspended by wire high in the air, beamed its light down onto the crèche. Our angel wings glistened as windblown tinsel sparkled in the light. The only sound now was the melodic strain of "Silent Night" emitting from the public address system.

For thirty minutes we remained frozen in position, each of us locked in private meditation.

I'm uncertain what prompted the extraordinary awakening I experienced at that moment. Perhaps it was Joseph's reaching over gently to calm the restless donkey or Mary's loving consolation of the baby in the manger.

Or was it the hushed crowd or the view of small children staring in wide-eyed wonder? Maybe it was the glimpse of cars pulling to the side of the roadway, sitting reverently, then quietly driving away.

Whatever caused it, our Nativity scene came to life for me that night. Christ's birth no longer seemed so distant. It was as if we truly were in Bethlehem, as if Baby Jesus, himself, was cooing in the manger. And there, right in front of my eyes, stood three wise men, bearing gifts for the Christ child.

For the first time, I *saw* those gifts, and in my reverie pondered the meaning of Gold, Frankincense, and Myrrh.

Gold. Gold is for a king. Only God could have told them that the tiny baby in the obscure stall is a King! I stood, awed, in the presence of royalty.

Frankincense, a sweet perfume. The Old Testament tells us that frankincense was offered in worship to God, and to God alone. These wise men accepted Jesus—cradle and all—as the Son of God! My own heart bowed before Him.

Myrrh. Strange that they should bring myrrh as a gift. Myrrh was one of the bitter spices used for burying the dead. It meant suffering. Even at His birth, the wise men were giving tribute to a Savior—one who was to be sacrificed.

Do angels cry? If so, do their tears freeze in the coldness of night?

As I stood beneath the star, I was overwhelmed with the vastness of God's love. Who but a loving Father would send such a sweet, precious *little Baby,* so we could know He came for *everyone*—even the helpless. And that He would send Him to such lowly surroundings so that we could know He came for *everyone*—even the poorest.

I felt a sudden urge to break ranks, to turn to the people and proclaim like the angels of old, "Behold, I bring you good tidings of great joy!" I wanted to call out," He's here! Jesus is truly here!"

Instead I gazed at the manger. *Sleep on, dear Holy Infant, sleep on. Sleep—in heavenly peace.*

The floodlights went out. But the effect of that night lingers still. For through the years my benediction echoes over and over in my heart. *Live on, dear Holy One, live on. Live on, dear Jesus—in me.*

Xena Finds a Home

*"God has two dwellings—one in heaven and
the other in a meek and thankful heart."*
Izaak Walton (1593-1683)
12,000 Religious Quotations

Sometimes God speaks to us in unexpected ways.

I answered the ringing phone that December day to hear the voice of Dr. Ford, our long-time veterinarian. "Mrs. Stargel," he said, "stop by and pick up your Christmas present."

My immediate thought: *Oh, I do hope it's not a cat.* My husband claims he doesn't care for cats. Even so, Joe had learned to love Misty, our beautiful silver-tipped Persian who lived with us for nineteen years. After age-related health problems claimed her, though, he was content to live without a cat. And in all honesty, I had about decided the same thing.

Dr. Ford had taken care of Misty all her life and officiated at her home going. At my request, he even made a house call to spare her the added trauma of going to the clinic. Upon observing my grief, Dr. Ford had said, "I want you to have one of my kittens. Come out to the truck and see my mama cat."

Swiping at my tears as we started out the front door, I said, "Joe doesn't want me to have another one. He says I get too attached to them, which I do."

"He wouldn't make you turn down a gift, would he?"

"He might," I said, admiring the beautiful charcoal-colored Persian he now held in his arms.

Still, that was five years ago. And besides, I never dreamed Dr. Ford *meant* it—that he actually intended to give me one of his Persians. In the past he and I had discussed books of mutual interest, so I told myself, *maybe it will just be a book.*

Next day after the phone call, I dropped by his animal clinic whereupon his young assistant came out carrying a little ball of charcoal fur with a pair of huge amber eyes. What could I do? Borrowing a carrying box, kitty food and a supply of litter, I headed home with the gift.

Spotting Joe working in the yard, I stopped the car in the driveway and called him over. "You'll never guess what's in the back seat."

He responded in a half-kidding tone, "It had better not be a cat."

All went downhill from there. To cinch the *not welcome* atmosphere at our house, the ball of fur turned out to be one rambunctious feline. So much so that I named her Xena, the Warrior Princess.

The term "curiosity killed the cat" must surely have been coined while observing one like Xena. Absolutely nothing was beyond her personal examination—not a fresh floral arrangement on the dining-room table, not collectibles on high bookshelves, not anything put on top of the refrigerator for safekeeping. Joe reminded me regularly, "You need to find a nice Christian home for that cat."

But as kittens will do, Xena began to steal hearts. Sometimes, she even honored me by snoozing in my lap. Or when completely exhausted from her activities, she would curl up in the out basket on my desk and sink into a deep sleep. She even took to rolling all over Joe's feet, inviting playtime. And who can resist marveling at the positions cats assume when completely relaxed—stretched out, top half turned in one direction, bottom half in the other?

One day, about three weeks after Xena's arrival, Joe comes in from shopping carrying a two-foot silk Christmas tree, decorated with miniature, glittering red packages. With a grin, he hands it to me. "You said Xena needs her own Christmas tree."

Having said nothing of the sort, I shake my head in disbelief. After placing the tree where Xena can attack it to her heart's content, Joe and I hold hands while we laugh at her antics as she checks out her new treasure.

Now wearing a grin of my own, I tell a happily busy cat: "Xena—Welcome Home!"

I can't help thinking, though, of that first Christmas. How Mary and Joseph must have felt when time came for her to deliver that precious little boy. Like Xena, they found no welcome mat out. I like to think I would have given baby Jesus *my* room at the Inn. But would I? Do I, even now? Do I always allow Him first place in my heart? In my life?

Perhaps, I tell myself as I ponder these things, *perhaps I need to stop my own busyness from time to time and declare anew:* "Jesus—Welcome Home!"

Me? A Dognapper?

"Joy is the echo of God's life within us."
Joseph Marmion, "Orthodoxy"
12,000 Religious Quotations

My unplanned venture into the canine underworld.

Ring-g-g-g-g-!!! I reach for the telephone and answer with a droopy "Hello."

"Gloria, this is Elizabeth. Would you like to go for a walk? The weather is gorgeous!"

Actually, no, I didn't want to go for a walk. For that matter I didn't want to do *anything.* Except maybe continue to mope about the house in my ratty old chenille robe, feeling all out-of-sorts. For like a deflated hot-air balloon, the joy had simply gone out of my day

Remembering, though, that I had half-heartedly mentioned my problem to God and maybe should be expecting His help, I respond, "I guess so, Elizabeth."

"Good. I'll drive over to your house and we'll start from there."

As soon as we step off our front porch, I realize her idea holds promise.

It is an afternoon in early November when the sun slants that peculiar angle that opens up an unblemished sapphire sky. The air is so crisp you can *smell* Fall—"football weather."

"Oh, by the way, Elizabeth," I say as we reach the street, "we'll have company for our walk."

Just then, from behind the magnolia next door, lumbers Coco, a huge black dog with long hair hiding her eyes. Coco, who looks and moves much like a half-grown grisly, has fancy French ancestry—Bouviers des Flandres. Now she woofs loudly as if to say to the two golden retrievers who live just beyond her, "Come on, you guys, Gloria's going for a walk today after all."

Whereupon Winston and Bubba come bounding up, brown eyes laughing in happy anticipation. Winston jostles my hand for his usual love pat—Bubba nudges my leg to tell me he has in his mouth the always-present tennis ball. "Want to play catch?" he grins. *Or is Winston the one with the tennis ball? Somehow, I've never been able to tell for sure which is which.*

"Watch this routine," I told Elizabeth. "First they'll inspect the Watson's yard. Then they'll cross the street to make sure the Stowe's mailbox is O.K. Then on to the little patch of woods at the end of the street to see if they can scare up a rabbit." As predicted, penny-colored Winston and Bubba—plume-like tails waving in unison—romp joyfully back and forth, rendezvousing with us from time to time to make sure we're still with them. Coco, meanwhile, possibly due to his sheep dog breeding, lopes along a little more cautiously but with obvious pleasure.

Their enthusiasm is contagious. Elizabeth and I decide to extend our walk over to "The Village," a subdivision on the other side of a major highway. No problem, though. The three dogs are well trained. They know they're not allowed to fight the traffic. "All right, you fellas," I tell them. "This is where you stop. We'll be back later." They obediently sit a moment by the telephone pole, their boundary marker. As I glance around

222

to check on them they reluctantly headed toward home, tails drooping.

Elizabeth and I keep walking, through one subdivision—then another. The sun warms our backs; the lingering reds and golds of autumn lure us on. A couple of hours pass before we turn around. About halfway back, a golden retriever appears at my side, his nose nudges my hand with an obvious "Am I glad to see you!"

"Oh, no, Winston!" I cradled the dog's gentle head between both my hands and look into soulful brown eyes. "Where did you come from?" Then my parental concern takes over. "Winston, I told you not to follow us. And where are the others?" *If something happened to them, it's all my fault. I knew I should have stayed home today.*

To the big furry creature leaning against me now, I said "Come on, boy. Stay close and I'll get you back across the highway." Winston happily obliges. Upon reaching the four-lane highway, I clutch his collar and guide him to safety.

Winston is excited. *He's glad to be back in familiar surroundings,* I'm thinking, as I mentally pat myself on the back. Winston sniffed out the rabbit patch. Then examined the Stowe's mailbox. From there we caught sight of my neighbors' front yards, the yards where the dogs live.

Wait a minute.

Sitting up there, anticipating our return, are Coco, and Bubba—*and* Winston! All three dogs!

Oh, oh!

I looked down at the huge copper-colored dog waiting patiently at my feet and ask, "Well, who are *you????*"

About that same moment, the trio on the hill spot this intruder. They take off after him like wild things. I yelled: "Cocoa, Bubba, Winston—stop that!!!" But their native instinct to protect home turf overrides their obedience training. I am still hollering "No! No! Come back here!" when my four-footed guest disappears behind the Martins' house on the corner, the trio in ears-laid-back pursuit.

Elizabeth leaves me at my house and I go inside to cook supper. But I couldn't get my mind off that dog. After all, I brought him over here. *What if they killed him? Or what if he was run over trying to get home?*

Finally, I could stand it no longer. I *have* to know. I cut off the burner under the potatoes and head down the street toward the heavily-traveled road. Fortunately the canine trio don't see me this time so I walk alone. And just as I reach the little clump of woods that edges the thoroughfare, from out of nowhere appears a warm, fuzzy nose nudging my hand. *"I knew you'd come back for me,"* the terrified dog seems to say.

Getting down on one knee, I hugged that big rascal. "Boy I'm glad to see you, too! And you're not hurt! Good boy. Good boy."

As I patted him, I noticed his collar has an I.D. tag. *Of course. Why didn't I think of that before?* "Let's see just who you are anyway, big fella."

Sure enough. The address on the tag is one Elizabeth and I passed earlier in the day. Embarrassed, I take hold of my new friend's collar, and lead him—once again across the highway—hoping against hope that no one sees us, I escort him back home. Mission accomplished, I sigh in relief, *Thank you, Jesus.*

As I hike the couple of miles back to where *I* belong, the humor of the situation hit me. I laugh out loud—a real guffaw! *Wait until I relate this little incident to Joe.* I imagine my husband's half-serious reaction. *He'll say: "I can just see the headlines now: JUDGE'S WIFE ARRESTED FOR DOGNAPPING!"*

And that's exactly what he said. While I doubled with laughter, picturing the instant I realized I had *three* golden retrievers when I was entitled to only *two*.

I learned a valuable lesson that day. Anytime I feel depressed, I need only ask God for help. Then get up and get going. Be receptive. He will bring into my path someone—or *something*—to restore the joy of living.

I still chuckle whenever I recall my escapade in the canine underworld. *Me! A Dognapper! It's too much.*

FOR OUR 50TH CLASS REUNION
GAINESVILLE HIGH SCHOOL
HOME OF THE RED ELEPHANTS

Remembering

At graduation, when hopes were high
and dreams for our futures
reached to the sky,
We went out into the waiting world
and lived—
and loved—
and possessions squirreled.

Like sand in an hourglass
the years dropped away,
too quickly—
too soon—
It's the future—today!

What have I done with the years
that were mine?
Made friends?
Served God?
Helped mankind?

"I've left nothing, done nothing
worthwhile," you say?
Don't despair—
tomorrow is another day—

time to say that kind word,
do that deed left undone,
smile that smile that will
lift another into the sun.

As you go, hold the love of
these friends from the past,
tho fun times of school days
surely won't last.
The joy of this evening
will fade soon, and yet,
take hope from our motto—

ELEPHANTS NEVER FORGET

Aloha Means "Hello"— and "Goodbye"

[Jesus said] "I have come that they may have life and have it to the full."
John 10:10b, NIV

With no current crisis, blessedly a time to play.

Randy phoned from his Atlanta office, "Mother, I'm going back to Hawaii next spring. Would you like to go?"

"Count me in!" I fairly shouted. "I've always wanted to see Hawaii."

Right away I started researching our Fiftieth State. In addition to facts and figures, I learned that even though almost everyone there speaks English, it helps—and is more fun—to know two key Hawaiian words: *mahalo* and *aloha*. *Mahalo* (mah-HAH-low) means "thank you." And *aloha* means much more than a simple "hello." It conveys trust and love, whether used as a greeting—or as a fond farewell.

We boarded a Delta L1011 for the nonstop flight from Atlanta to Honolulu. Traveling with the two of us were my friend Gloria and my nephew Tom. After nine long hours, with the Pacific Ocean stretching from horizon to horizon, Randy pointed out the plane's window, "There's our island!"

I gulped. "You don't mean we're expected to land on that that little dark spot down there!"

"I'm afraid so," he said. "That's Oahu."

Fortunately the island grew a bit larger as we got closer. I appreciated, too, that our approach flew over the Pearl Harbor Memorial. A reverent hush fell among the passengers as we remembered the thousands of young men who lost their lives on that infamous day, December 7, 1941.

After landing at the modern, bustling airport in Honolulu, we flew in a Hawaiian Air DC9 to the island actually *named* Hawaii, known as "The Big Island."

THE BIG ISLAND

Our plane taxied to a stop at the Keahole Airport and we struggled with carry-on luggage down a flight of steps to the tarmac. We three novices exclaimed in unison, "There's no terminal!"

Randy, obviously pleased with our reaction, ushered us over to several small, open-air, thatched-roof structures, each draped with blooming bougainvillea. Our introduction to the laid-back lifestyle of the Islands had begun. A lifestyle that proves highly contagious.

Here, where men as well as women, drape their necks with fragrant floral lei, we could hardly wait to slip into the flowered shirts and flowing muumuus, and to tuck a red hibiscus behind the ear.

Forcing our many bags into the rented station wagon (all of us, except Randy, had over packed), we set out for our destination, Mauna Lani Resort. Even though Randy had cautioned we would drive through twenty miles of "moonscape," I was not prepared for the utter desolation. As far as eye could see—acres and acres of black, centuries-old volcanic lava.

"This is just another of the many contrasts of Hawaii," Randy explained. "Most of the island is green. Yearly rainfall varies according to area, from six inches to three hundred."

Mauna Lani was a welcome oasis. There—on top of lava fields—man had worked with nature's iridescent ocean and wonderfully pleasant trade winds to create a tropical paradise. I was mesmerized by the swaying palm trees, beautiful beaches, and variegated ocean. Especially the ocean. Shades of turquoise near the shore give way to deep sapphire further out, leaving one awed by the richness of God's artistry.

The resort features, too, an award-winning restaurant, *The Canoe House*. Picture it: Our first night on Hawaii we're sitting on a lanai by the Pacific ocean, watching a picturesque sunset over distant Maui, listening to live Hawaiian singing, cooking our own appetizers on a 500-degree rock brought to the table, dining on unbelievably-delicious Polynesian food, and experiencing—for the first time—those gentle trade winds. We four sat there with jet-lag bleary eyes, grinned at each other, and agreed: "It doesn't get much better than this."

We spent our first week headquartered at Mauna Lani—beach bums and pool pods by morning, sightseers by afternoon, and by evening: diners in colorful muumuus and decorated shirts, trying out all the top-rated restaurants at nearby resorts.

One such restaurant was at the Hyatt Regency Waikoloa. "You have to see this hotel to believe it," Randy said. He was right. We decided it was a mixture of a Walt Disney and a Cecil B. DeMille production! In the elegant lobby, of all places, we boarded a small boat for an enchanting night cruise through the gardens and by the shops! Also in the lobby, you can catch a tram if you prefer rail travel to your room.

A LAND OF CONTRASTS

Hawaii is called the "Big Island" because it is almost twice the combined size of all the other Hawaiian Islands—yet it is only 93 X 76 miles. Even so, it offers—besides volcanic deserts and ocean-swept coastlines—the contrasts of tropical valleys, snow-capped mountains and rolling pasturelands. It boasts the second largest privately owned ranch in the United States—22,000 acres. And Kona coffee, and orchid farms, and the Macadamia Nut Factory, and ... so much to see.

And so captivating. After being there a few days, even the barrenness of a lava field takes on a beauty of it own.

From our rented condominium, we could see the majestic mountains of Hawaii—Mauna Kea (13,796 feet) and Mauna Loa (13,677 feet). Both are volcanoes, providing the most dramatic contrast of them all. For Mauna Kea is considered inactive while Mauna Loa is *very* active. (Read the effects of Mauna Loa's volcanic activity in Chapter 3, "Death of a Village.)

"Mauna Kea is called White Mountain," I read aloud from the coffee-table book, "because sub-freezing temperatures often cover it in snow. Adventurous skiers can take four-wheel vehicles to the summit to enjoy the thrill of its steep slopes. Two hours later they can be swimming in the 75-degree waters of the Pacific."

Atop Mauna Kea, too, sits the Mauna Kea Observatory, an important link in the worldwide surveillance of the stars and planets. The observatory is above forty percent of the earth's atmosphere, providing a vividly clear window to the mysteries of the universe.

Among our tours, I found the Waipi'o Valley especially fascinating. We took the necessary four-wheel drive vehicle down into this "Valley of the Kings." I imagined how it might have been when King Kamahameha, the much-loved ruler who unified the Islands, grew up there. Now, wild horses roam freely among the banana and papaya trees, the towering waterfalls,

231

and crystal rivers. Only a half dozen families still live and tend their taro fields in Waipi'o.

LIVING A LUAU

On my list of things to do in Hawaii, top priority was a luau. It remains my most cherished memory of the trip. At the Regency Waikoloan, the luau lived up to my dreams—from the first blowing of the conch shell and the ceremonious lighting of torches, to the unearthing of the roasted pig.

As the setting sun put on its own show, we gathered on the beach to partake of forty-five sumptuous native dishes. Here we sampled *poi*—a staple of the Hawaiian diet—a bland "paste-like" dish made from pounded taro roots, a tasty accompaniment to pork or fish. After the feast, dancers and musicians in native dress put on a lively show with the intriguing chants and graceful dances of ancient Hawaii.

One fun sidelight: Earlier that evening, we had just arrived for the luau when Randy and Tom went ahead to reconnoiter the area. Strolling along the beautifully landscaped gardens, Gloria and I happened upon a TV crew, shooting scenes with former Olympic champion Bruce Jenner for an upcoming show, *Healthy Lifestyles.* The next thing we knew, the director invited us to act as extras. Hams that we are, we just jumped right in there. I wish I had a photo of Randy's and Tom's expressions when they returned a few minutes later and found the two of us being televised, *acting* with Bruce Jenner!

OAHU

We flew back to Oahu for the last three days of our trip. There contrasts continued. We went from the almost-private highways on the Big Island to bumper-to-bumper traffic in Honolulu. Besides cars, people were *everywhere* and high-rise hotels crowded upon one another.

THE PINK PALACE

Yet in the midst of the congestion and asphalt jungle, there exists yet another oasis, another tropical paradise—the world-famous landmark of Waikiki, *The Royal Hawaiian.* Only six stories high, it is one of only a handful of hotels that actually front the *Waikiki Beach.* In its carefully maintained gardens stand stately palms that were set out by King Kamahameha, himself.

Many sailors who served in the Pacific during the war remember The Royal Hawaiian, known as "The Pink Palace." From 1941 to 1945 the Navy took over the hotel and used it as a rest-and-relaxation center for the men returning from battle.

The hotel was built in 1927 to entertain wealthy tourists who came over on the luxury cruise liners. The historic Pink Palace, only recently restored to its original old-world grandeur, made us feel like royalty. From our fifth floor picture windows, we looked out on the incredibly lovely water. To our left, Diamond Head crater stood sculptured against the blue Hawaii sky. And, at night, over all that, a full moon. Awesome!

"I agree it's difficult to leave here for even a day," Randy said, "but there is one other place you must see." A thirty-mile ride up the coast took us to the Polynesian Cultural Center. There, villages have been recreated representing the seven different homelands from which the first Polynesians came to the Hawaiian Islands. Natives from each of the villages showed us something of their carefree, happy lives before civilization moved in. At one village, they taught us to dance the hula. Perhaps I should say they *tried* to teach us.

That night, natives put on an indescribable extravaganza! "This is Polynesia" was so beautiful it brought tears to my eyes. For, in truth, much of the Islands' charm comes from their people—and from the way things used to be.

MAHALO — AND ALOHA

Too soon, the day came when we must head back to the mainland. But the four of us had lost our hearts to Hawaii. We didn't want to leave. Besides, we hadn't even touched the islands of Maui, nor Kauai, nor Molokai. "There is only one thing to do," I said, fighting an urge to cry. "We must come back some day."

So, to you, Hawaii, I say: "Mahalo."

And to your gentle people: "Aloha—until we meet again."

CHAPTER 7

Jesus, Our Power

He Is the Wind Beneath Our Wings

When you come to the edge
of all the light you've known
And are about to step off into the
darkness of the unknown,
Faith is knowing one of two things will happen:
There will be something solid to stand on
Or you will be taught how to fly.

Author Unknown

Captured— Never Defeated

As written for: Ben Purcell,
Colonel, U. S. Army, Retired

*[Jesus said] "My grace is sufficient for thee: for my
strength is made perfect in weakness."*
2 Corinthians 12:9a, KJV

P.O.W: Five years in solitary confinement. They might take his freedom, but with God's help, they would not take his spirit.

Until that moment, the day had loomed long and depressing, same as all the others. A prisoner of war, I had already been held captive in North Vietnam for two years, in total isolation, not allowed to see or speak to another human being except my captors when they took me out of my cell for interrogation. I was allowed nothing to relieve the endless hours. Nothing to read. Not even anything on the bleak walls.

I missed my wife and five young children terribly. Allowed no communication, they didn't know if I were alive or dead. I worried about their welfare, and I knew they worried about me.

From the outset—ever since our helicopter was shot down—the principle goal of my captors apparently was to break my spirit. They'll never know just how close they came.

That particular afternoon, though something bright and shiny came skipping under the door of my cramped cell and bounced off the back wall. It was a piece of hard candy, wrapped in gold foil! Who would dare to risk harsh punishment by befriending me? Whoever it was, this brave gesture brightened my spirit beyond words.

I made the piece of candy last until it was nearly dark outside. Then I realized I had a bonus: a small piece of gold foil. I took the foil, fashioned it in the shape of a mountain, and hung it on the wall just beneath the new bamboo Cross I had made. I wanted something—anything—to break up the blankness of my existence.

It was beautiful. I watched the light play upon it, then split off into little golden beams. Because of the Cross, I could make this into the hill of Calvary and with very little imagination, see the crucifixion as it must have been played out 2,000 years ago. Sometimes, I would put my hands around my eyes, like blinders, and slowly sweep my gaze across the wall until the gold foil came into view. I would watch it in the evening until the light was too dim to see, and be greeted by it in the morning when the room grew light.

My mood began to pick up. Two days after I put the piece of foil on the wall, a turnkey entered my cell and removed both the foil and the cross. I was devastated. Why did they take them away? What harm could a little piece of foil and a bamboo cross be?

I lay on my bunk for the rest of the day, mourning the loss of my "interest center." I actually found myself crying.

Then I told myself that this was getting out of hand. There was no way I was going to make it through if I let everything effect me as this had. I had to do something positive to help my own cause. So I went on a hunger strike.

I knew that whatever convoluted logic it was that guided these people, they could better explain a death from beating than from starvation. I eventually won a half-victory when they compromised. "You can have the cross back," the guard growled, "but you cannot have that piece of paper."

All this time, even during periods of depression like this one, I had greeted each sunrise as a new day of hope. *This is the day that peace will come to this war-torn land. This is the day of your freedom, Ben. This is the day you'll be going home.*

Then, as the sun set that evening and I found myself still in prison, I would say *Tomorrow will be here soon, and tomorrow will bring peace.*

Today, though, I honestly was beginning to wonder if I would ever be free again.

For the hundredth time, maybe the thousandth—my tortured thoughts replayed my one night of freedom six months earlier—the night I'd escaped.

It had taken the first year to learn that this prison compound was located about six miles from Hanoi. At the precise moment I learned where I was, I made my decision to attempt an escape.

The question was, of course, how to get out of my cell—then the prison—then North Vietnam, each obstacle exponentially more difficult than the one before.

For three months I studied the situation.

There was no window to my cell, but there were bars in the top half of the door, and wooden shutters that covered the bars. The shutters were sometimes left open during the day so I could look out in the courtyard. They were closed at night and anytime there was another prisoner in the yard.

The bottom half of the door was made of hard wood, more than one inch thick.

Wood!

Woodworking was one of my hobbies, and I had worked with all sorts of wood. *If I had the tools,* I figured, *I could fashion a removable panel on that door.*

I decided I would *make* the tools. But with what? Furnishings in my cell consisted of only two items: the bunk and a toilet bucket in the corner.

However, several pieces of wire were embedded in the plaster wall, put there so we could hang mosquito netting at night. I dug a piece of this wire out by using a bamboo sliver, then made a drill by bending the wire around a bamboo handle.

For a chisel, I found an extra sixpenny nail in my bunk. It took a couple days of working it back and forth, but I got it out. I flattened the nail by dragging it across the concrete floor. I started work. It was a slow process, partly because of the inefficient tools, and partly because I had to drill a few seconds, then listen for the guards, then drill another few seconds. And that's where my "watch-chicken" came in.

There were chickens clucking and cackling and scratching around the yard all the time. When the shutters were open, I liked to watch them, just to pass the time. There was one rooster I particularly enjoyed. He was the cockiest little thing you ever saw, strutting around like he owned the world.

One day I threw a breadcrumb out to him and he came over to eat it. He was entertaining, so I started throwing out a few crumbs after each meal. In return he developed the habit of hanging around my door. Then, one day, the little rooster squawked and ran away. A moment later, the guard walked by. When the guard was gone, the rooster came back. *Ah-hah!* My mind clicked. A *"watch-chicken!"*

So it was that a North Vietnamese rooster was recruited for the United States Army. With the rooster standing watch for me, I tripled my work speed.

"Rooster," I said, speaking so quietly that not even the chicken just outside my door could hear me. "What is the *Fifth General Order?*"

I answered for him. "Sir, my Fifth General Order is to quit my post only when properly relieved."

"Very good," I said, working out another splinter of wood. "See that you remember that. Oh, and maybe you'd better get a haircut before tomorrow's inspection."

As I played the silly little game of guard mount with the rooster, I continued to work, and as I worked, I planned the next stage of the operation.

After another three months of intense effort, I was ready. That night, at 10 P.M., I prayed a quick little prayer. "Lord, help me in my time of danger. Fill my heart with the courage to face the unknown one more time. Amen."

I made it past the perimeter wall, dodging the broken glass imbedded on top as well as the electric wires strung above it. Sadly, however, the next morning found me in a police station in Hanoi, being held until the Camp Commander with a number of guards appeared to take me back to the prison.

As punishment, I lay on a solid board bunk with my ankles in stocks for the next two weeks. I was uncomfortable and in pain, but I was *not* depressed. In fact, I would say my mood was almost buoyant. At least I had *tried* to escape. For the first time since my capture, I felt alive! I had regained my self-respect, something that had vanished when I surrendered after the helicopter crash. I was alive and well. I was glad I did it, and vowed that if another opportunity presented itself, I would do it again.

For the time being, I resolved that whenever I needed a day brightener, I would recall that little piece of foil-wrapped candy and the brave act of kindness it represented. It gave me courage to vow yet again: *They might take my freedom, but with God's help, they will not take my spirit.*

AUTHOR'S NOTE: Portions of this story adapted from their book, *Love and Duty*, by Anne and Ben Purcell, used by permission of the authors. The Purcell's live in Clarksville, Georgia, surrounded by their Christmas Tree Farm. On the front of their garage flies a large American flag and painted beneath—in bold red letters—is the message:

Man's most precious possession, second only to life itself, is freedom.

The enemy held Col. Purcell in solitary confinement three more years, but they never took his spirit. He did pull off another escape: this time he eluded the heavily armed search party 30 hours. When finally peace came, he learned he had been the highest-ranking army officer held P.O.W.

Destination: Bottom of the World

As written for: Oscar T. Cassity,
Major, U.S. Air .Force, Retired

"The wings of prayer carry high and far."
Anonymous

We go along on a history-making mission.

When Navy officers showed me a D-2 Caterpillar tractor, modified with wide tracks for snow, I shook my head in disbelief. The monster machine weighed 12,700 pounds! *They want me to airdrop that thing?! At the South Pole?! "OPERATION DEEP FREEZE" indeed!*

Usually I welcomed a new challenge. I was 31, a seasoned— and maybe even a little cocky—Air Force pilot. I had already flown combat missions in Europe, tight flights for the Berlin Air Lift, and combat missions in Korea. Even so, that morning in 1955, at Naval Air Station Quonset Point, Rhode Island, I knew I had met my match.

Weeks earlier, at Donaldson Air Force Base in Greenville, South Carolina, where I was stationed, word had come down from 18th Air Force brass: "In preparation for the International

243

Geophysical Year of 1957, the United States plans to construct the first permanent scientific station at the South Pole. The Navy will do the building. Our job is to deliver and airdrop everything—500 tons of building material, fuel, food and scientific supplies."

Next came the clincher: "Aerial delivery operations officer for OPERATION DEEP FREEZE: Capt. Oscar T. Cassity."

No problem, I had thought at the time. Now it was obvious this operation would be no picnic. Still, all my life, with the Lord's help, I had tackled the impossible.

At 15, my 17-year-old brother and I dug a well in North Georgia's hard red clay. By hand! Months of hard labor and thirty-five feet deep later—we struck water!

Joining the Air Force just out of high school, I heard, "You'll never get into pilot training without a college degree." I failed the first try, but applied again. And earned my wings. In the upper 10% of my class. By age 21, I was flying combat.

Then there was the Yugoslavia mission. My orders had me fly a small plane behind enemy lines to rescue a group of displaced persons, who faced almost certain death if caught by the Nazis. I landed in the designated miniscule pasture and found waiting, instead of the expected twenty-six passengers, forty desperate souls. I simply didn't have room for more than twenty-six, yet I couldn't leave even one behind. I flew them to safety, even though our overloaded little plane brushed treetops coming out.

My conclusion: *Difficult jobs just mean I have to try harder—and pray more.* Besides, with the whole world still recovering from two devastating wars, it was encouraging to learn that twelve nations were joining together in a *peaceful* project—to conduct research on the continent of Antarctica. *So,* I reasoned, *if the Navy needs that D2 Caterpillar to prepare the building site at the South Pole ...* I returned to Donaldson and set about to carry out my assignment for OPERATION DEEP FREEZE.

At that time, our jumbo military transport—the C124 Globemaster—was the only plane with the necessary range and cargo capacity to accomplish the mission. There was a major problem, though: nothing as heavy as the D2 ever had been dropped from a C124.

In fact, the Globemaster was not designed for large airdrops. True enough, it could hold a Greyhound bus. But the vehicles it transported rolled in and out—on the ground.

Besides, the inhospitable target area itself presented problems not covered in the rulebook. I would need to devise new rules to fit the new requirements.

I gathered the top non-commissioned officers of the 1st Aerial Port Squadron for a series of brainstorming sessions. "Men, here's what we have to do. First and foremost is the matter of an adequate platform on which to mount the D2 tractor for airdropping. There exists a 6,000-pound load-bearing platform, but it is designed for rearward extraction. We need downward ejection. Plus the D2 weighs over twice that limit."

Together, the men and I came up with a set of plans to construct an H-frame adapter that would fit the elevator up locks of the C124; then had the adapter manufactured.

Meantime, we figured the drop would require a parachute at each corner of the platform or the Caterpillar would yo-yo around out there.

After months of rigging adjustments and test drops of similar-weighted materials, in October, I flew back up to Quonset Point for a do-or-die test drop of the real thing.

On the day of the drop, back at Donaldson Air Base, the 18th Air Force Commander called a staff meeting which reportedly went like this: "Gentlemen," the General announced, "I hold in my right hand this notice from the Douglas Aircraft Manufacturer: 'Without extensive and costly modifications to the aircraft, a D2 Caterpillar tractor cannot be dropped from a C124.' Yet," the General continued, "in my left hand I hold a strike report: 'This afternoon, at Quonset Point, RI, Capt.

Oscar T. Cassity successfully airdropped a D2 Caterpillar tractor from his C124.'"

Among the squadron, it became an oft-repeated punchline: "The general forgot to tell the captain it couldn't be done."

Our successful test drop signaled "Mission Go." The Air Force could deliver everything necessary for OPERATION DEEP FREEZE.

Even so, we still faced further obstacles, unanswered questions, and even a few mishaps. We knew the hostile environment of Antarctica—the highest, coldest, and windiest elevation in the world—could detrimentally affect our equipment.

Searching for similar conditions, I arranged test drops in snow-covered Leadville, Colorado, and watched from the ground as my men dropped six tons of sand-and-water-filled barrels—and inadvertently draped huge silk parachutes over high-tension wires, knocking out power all over the Hoover Dam area.

On takeoff the next day, another pilot had just become airborne when the huge plane's left main landing gear hit a snow bank and the C124 plummeted back to earth. Fortunately, no one was injured, but it crippled the plane. Donaldson had to send out another Globemaster to bring us home.

I had my answers, at least, regarding cold and velocity. One vital observation: with the available parachute-disconnect system, high winds would drag the dropped equipment across unreachable expanses of ice. Or if the chutes detached too soon, the equipment would disappear into deep snow.

The men and I designed two quick-release devices and had them manufactured: for the D2 Caterpillar, an electrically actuated explosive charge upon contact with the surface; for the standard drop bundle, a preset timing device.

Following more months of modifications and testing came the long, long flight from Greenville to the bottom of the world. Hawaii. The Fiji Islands. And finally Christchurch, New Zealand, the operational base.

In November 1956, OPERATION DEEP FREEZE in Antarctica got underway. With 24-hour daylight during the four summer months, we planned round-the-clock rotation, airdropping supplies at the South Pole. For the round trip of over 1600 miles, eight C124 Globemasters would fly from the only airstrip on the continent: a 14-foot-deep floating ice shelf permanently attached to the continent at McMurdo Sound.

Meanwhile, a ski-equipped Navy Dakota made an exploratory first landing at the Pole. Successful, they ferried in their construction crews.

The day of reckoning came. My Globemaster lifted off the ice shelf at McMurdo. The D2 Caterpillar, trussed up tight like a giant caged bird, dominated the cavernous cargo bay.

Below us, Antarctica—larger than Europe or Australia—stretched white and empty as far as the eye could see. No living creature anywhere. The ice-encased continent, still largely unexplored—with its treacherous terrain of man-swallowing crevasses and its weather of biting cold, fierce winds and sudden blizzards, even during its short summer—leaves the adventurer no margin for error. On land, or in the air.

And somewhere near the middle of the continent—on a 10,000-foot-high plateau—lies the Geographic South Pole.

After hours of flying, we were there. I took a deep breath. *Please, God, everything rests on this drop.* I lowered our altitude and slowed our speed. The big doors under the plane's belly opened. The bundled-up D2 ejected with a gigantic swoosh. In its place, a blast of 50-below-zero air gushed into the aircraft.

Seconds later, I viewed one of the prettiest sights I've ever seen: four 100-foot parachutes floating straight down to the target. They disconnected as planned.

I banked and circled back, flying low. On the ground below, the bright yellow Caterpillar chugged happily across frozen terrain, five navy crewmen aboard yelling and giving us thumbs up.

Flying there at the bottom of the globe, I switched on the intercom for a heading. "Mr. Navigator, how do we get out of here?"

His answer by now has become classic, "Just head north, Sir."

The crew burst into tension-relieving laughter at our navigator-turned-comedian. Finally, he told us *which* north.

When the building down there was completed, a few hardy souls wintered over for the first time. Still today, important year-round scientific research continues at the Amundsen-Scott South Pole Station.

Although unique, my South Pole experience "does not of me a hero make." Like countless other veterans, I was given a job to do. And—with the help of some fine men and the good Lord—I just did it.

Even though they said it couldn't be done.

NOTE: Major O. T. Cassity passed away in May, 2006, and was buried with full military honors. The flyby of a vintage airplane gave the fitting, final salute to this one who deeply loved his country and was justly proud of his twenty-one years of service as a pilot in the United States Air Force.

A Winner — in More Ways Than One

*"But they that wait upon the LORD shall
renew their strength; they shall mount up with wings
as eagles; they shall run, and not be weary;
they shall walk, and not faint."*
Isaiah 40:31, KJV

She runs for those who can't.

It's a March morning with promise at Lake Lanier Islands in north Georgia.

At this serene lakeside resort, where dogwood trees are just beginning to unfurl their snow-white blossoms throughout the woods, the sun has broken through the early-morning haze to reveal a clear-blue sky.

Carefully groomed beds of tulips, red and gold, line the racecourse where Marine Corps Reservists are conducting a 10K run in support of the Shepherd Spinal Center, the regional spinal cord injury center located in Atlanta. We have just reached that critical time between the completion of the race and the posting of winners.

Some of the runners are milling about, cooling down, while others are stretching their muscles after the grueling 6.2 miles of hilly terrain. One perspiration-soaked young lady, blonde hair clinging to her forehead, hands thrust into her blue warm-up jacket, stands next to me in the pavilion, gazing at an incredible view of Lake Sidney Lanier.

"Beautiful, isn't it?" I venture, while filling paper cups with water. Just for today, I enjoy my role as "water person"—a help to my Marine Reservist husband.

"Yes, it certainly is," she agrees, almost reverently, as she begins to catch her breath.

Several athletes, stopping by to accept my proffered cups of water, divert my attention. They nod their thanks and move on.

The young blonde is still lost in contemplation.

"My name is Gloria. What's yours?" I inquire.

"Susan," she responds with a smile.

"Where are you from, Susan?"

"Gainesville."

Naturally curious, I feel compelled to ask, "Have you raced here before?"

Walking closer, Susan stands right in front of me, as if she is about to reveal a confidence. "I work as a physical therapist aide at Lanier Park Hospital," she says. "This is the third time I've run this race, but I never fully appreciated just *why* I was running until the other day." Susan pauses, her compassionate blue eyes filling with tears. "Recently I started working with some patients that the Shepherd Spinal Center sent to our hospital in Gainesville for rehabilitation."

I begin to understand why Susan is so pensive. Spinal cord injuries are always serious, often leaving their victims unable to walk, let alone run.

"I keep thinking about those patients," Susan says, as if reading my thoughts. "They would give almost anything to be out here. One young man, I'll call him Bill, was the star athlete at his high school—played baseball, football—until an automobile accident." Susan's face mirrors her concern. "Now he is paralyzed from the waist down, trying desperately just to learn how to walk again."

After a moment Susan continues, "Yesterday, I had just helped Bill back to his wheelchair after a grueling session at the parallel bars. He was completely spent. As I started out the door, word got around that I was running today. Bill called out all the way across the physiotherapy room, 'Bring me one of the T-shirts.'

"But I'm going to do even better than that," Susan eagerly confides. "If I win the trophy, I'm going to take it to Bill and our other patients. I'm going to present it to the department in their honor. I want to share it with them because they've worked so hard and have come so far. *They* are the real winners," she concludes, gesturing with both arms.

"What a beautiful story," I reply. "Mind if I print it?" Susan, wearing a furrowed brow and quizzical look, acknowledges me with an affirmative nod. She didn't imagine that this jeans-clad woman, in tennis shoes and red windbreaker bearing the Marine Corps emblem, happens to be a writer.

Suddenly a flurry of boisterous activity signals the beginning of the award presentations in the pavilion. I hear Marine Lt. Col. Mike Campbell announce through the megaphone, "First Female Finisher: Susan Edge!"

A round of applause rings out as a radiant Susan, blue warm-up jacket tied securely around her waist, enthusiastically steps forward, shakes the Lt. Colonel's hand, and receives her trophy—*their* trophy.

From the sidelines, I am moved almost to tears as within my heart I make my own personal presentation: Susan Edge—a winner—in more ways than one.

Call of the Canal

As written for: Margaret Culberson

"The LORD will watch over your coming and going
both now and forevermore."
Psalm 121.8, NIV

He'd always wanted to show her the Panama Canal. She would take this trip for him, as well as for herself.

That bright January afternoon, aboard the magnificent cruise ship *The Galaxy*, it was with mixed emotions—of anticipation and apprehension—that I watched the Galveston, Texas, dock become smaller and smaller, and the Gulf of Mexico waters become larger and larger.

Yet, from the moment several weeks earlier when I pulled the travel brochure from my mailbox, I knew I had to take this trip. I had rushed back into the house and phoned each of our three daughters: "Guess where I'm going next month!" Before any could answer, I sang out: "To the Panama Canal!"

"You're going to see 'Bob's Canal'?" each responded, dumbfounded. "You'd go without Dad, after you two talked all these years about seeing the canal *together*?"

"Yes, I *have* to go," I answered. "He wanted so much to show me his canal."

"But, Mother," each questioned, in one way or another, "that's a long, tiring trip to Central America! And besides, won't it be terribly difficult emotionally?"

"No doubt. But your dad would want me to go. I will do it for him, as well as for me."

Bob had served as a Merchant Seaman during World War II and made many trips through the Panama Canal, ferrying supplies to our troops in the Atlantic as well as the Pacific theatres of operation. During our fifty-seven years of marriage, he often spoke of his feelings each time his ship went through the locks of the canal. It was almost a sacred thing to him. And he would always add, "Margaret, I've just got to show you that canal."

In fact, the family heard it so often we referred to it lovingly as "Bob's Canal." I can still hear him saying, in a tone that indicated it was almost too good to be true, "Margaret, it's an engineering marvel. It can get your ship from the Atlantic to the Pacific in 8 hours! Before the canal was built, ships had to sail around the tip of South America to get to the same place!"

Then he'd add, "Wait until you see those locks. Truly ingenious."

Since it does require a long voyage to sail to Panama, we had delayed going until Bob retired. But he became ill and was never again well enough to make the trip. "Margaret," he had said, even then, "you must see the canal."

During Bob's long illness, we had said to each other all that needed to be said. When he died three years ago, there were no regrets, no unfinished business. Except one. I hadn't seen his canal.

So it was with some apprehension that I approached this trip. Would it be too painful to endure, seeing the canal without Bob?

I hadn't considered what memories the ship itself would evoke. After all, this was *his* world. Seeing the crews at work reminded me of how Bob looked when first we met—handsome indeed in his white uniform. He never lost that handsomeness. Or his sense of adventure. And as he had always done, he encouraged me to continue to stay busy with fun, interesting activities. I had done that. So busy I wouldn't have time to think, to grieve. Now, on board, I couldn't help but think.

One night, as I stood on the veranda outside our stateroom, loneliness engulfed me, loneliness as heavy as the fog that rolled in off the Caribbean Sea. Our Captain sounded the ship's foghorn and was answered by the mournful sounds of other foghorns on ships out there *somewhere*. I could feel the homesickness Bob and the other sailors must have felt many nights. *Lord,* I prayed, *did I do the right thing, coming on this trip?*

Everywhere, I saw reminders of Bob. As the deck hands manned the large machines that shot the mooring ropes out and brought them back in, I could hear Bob telling how he and the other young sailors had worked the lines the hard way—by hand.

Even so, he loved the sea and considered making it his career. However, when we married, he said, "It would be unfair to you to be married to someone gone all the time." Still, he kept his love of water and while rearing the three girls, we took them on many camping trips, fishing trips, and beach trips. As long as he had water to look at, swim in, or fish in, Bob was happy.

I hadn't fully realized how much Bob's sea experiences had become an integral part of our family's experiences until now. I shared with my roommate, Betty Jane: "In the Girl Scouts, when it came to knot-tying, our girls could beat out all the others; they could beat out most of the *guys* when it came to playing cribbage. And to this day," I told her, "we all pack our bags by rolling clothes into tight bundles like they did on the boat to take less space in their sea bags." Lord *as painful as the memories are, they bring a smile, too. Thank you.*

Bob's teachings came in handy, too, when I explained shipboard jargon. "Now, Betty Jane," I kidded, "remember: We don't say *left,* we say *portside,* and instead of *right,* it's *starboard.* Then there's *forward* and *aft* and *go below* and *stand watch.*" I impressed everyone within hearing distance during our mandatory lifeboat drill.

Another bittersweet memory surfaced: Through the years, Bob and I had taken several short cruises, and he would always have fun when he met the Captain. He'd say, "I just want you to know I'm available to help if you need me to take the ship out and again when docking."

Now, on this cruise, I couldn't resist. As soon as I met the Captain of The Galaxy I told him, "I'll be glad to help you get the ship in or out." I could almost hear Bob say, *"Way to go, Margaret."*

We made two ports-of-call on the way to Panama and although I enjoyed learning to prepare Mexican cuisine in Cozumel and touring Mayan ruins in Costa Maya, each day I returned early to the ship, eager to get underway. I wanted to see Bob's Canal.

Conversations on ship centered on the Panama Canal and its origin. I would choke up remembering the times Bob and I had sat around the kitchen table, talking about the engineering feats involved in building the canal. Although painful, I was beginning to see that every memory exposed an open emotional wound that needed air to heal.

Still, I was intrigued with the canal's history—the fact that its completion in 1914 represented the realization of a 400-year dream, ever since Balboa trudged weeks through the Panamanian jungle to discover the Pacific Ocean. Spain tried to build a passageway between the two oceans. Later France tried and failed, then sold the rights to the United States. Constructing the fifty-mile canal, with its many hardships and engineering nightmares, cost France and the United States $352,000,000 and 30,000 lives.

I thought it interesting, too, that ships going through the canal must pay a toll based on weight. The highest one was $141,344.91. The smallest was 36 cents, paid by a man who swam the canal in 1928.

The more I learned, the more eager I became to see the canal, especially those famous locks—to see them operate.

One night, after five days at sea, the public address system came to life with the Captain's announcement: "Ladies and Gentlemen," he began, in a tone of great importance, "Tomorrow, at 5:00 o'clock in the morning, The Galaxy will reach the Panama Breakwater. And then—the thing you've all come to see—the Panama Canal!"

We're almost there! I couldn't sleep. Long before the appointed hour, I stood on our veranda waiting, watching.

Finally—a faint light appeared on the horizon. Then, with dramatic flair, the Master Producer of All Things Beautiful pulled back the night curtains. And—there it was! The Panama Canal! Bob's Canal! A man-made concrete wonder framed by dense green jungle. I was awestruck. I felt I was dreaming.

Soon Panamanian crews boarded *The Galaxy* to pilot us through the canal. I leaned over the railing to watch, not wanting to miss a thing. As we entered the Gatun Locks and cut our power, they attached cables from our ship to mechanical "mules" on the tracks alongside. These mules, which looked like tiny toy trains, pulled our 886 ft. ship into and through the 1.6-mile long locks, raising us in three lock steps a total of 85 feet!

It was the most amazing thing I have ever experienced. The sensation of seeing the water rise and feeling our boat slowly lift upward is something I can't describe. I felt Bob standing there beside me saying, *See, I told you it was a magical thing.*

Filled with sadness, gladness, nervousness and awe, I became a blubbering mess. "Betty Jane," I managed between sobs, "it's a good thing the Captain doesn't need me today to help get our ship through the *canal*."

We resumed power into Gatun Lake, and anchored there for the night—Gatun Lake, one of the largest man-made bodies of water in the world.

Then it was through the narrow nine-mile Gaillard Cut to the Pedro Miguel and Miraflores Locks. Again—as gently as a mother lays her baby down to sleep—in three steps, twenty-five or thirty feet at a time, they lowered our 77,713 tons back down to sea level. *Awesome!*

Once more, our ship resumed power when suddenly—the climax, the finale! The Master Producer again pulled back the curtains, this time curtains of blocked view. And there—stretching out before me as far as the eye could see was—the Pacific Ocean! Incredible! *We did it, Bob! We did it!*

I knew a little of how Balboa must have felt when he first viewed that vast expanse of water. The exhilaration! In my head, I heard Bob's voice, *I am so proud of you, Margaret.*

As I stood mesmerized, his presence lingered. *Isn't the Panama Canal all I said it would be, Margaret?*

Even more so, Bob. Even more so.

I stayed there a long while, savoring every moment. For I knew I would treasure this memory forever. Now I saw more clearly than ever how God had blessed Bob and me with a wonderful marriage. One that had given me the courage to venture out and the freedom to again enjoy life.

I had answered the Call of the Canal. I was ready to go home.

The Gift

[*Jesus said*] *"For where two or three are gathered
together in my name, there am I in the midst of them."*
Matthew 18:20, KJV

Gifted musician learns a church is
more than a building.

Heartsick, Alice Oglesby wasn't prepared for the loss she
felt when she reached the demolition site of Atlanta's
historic First Baptist Church on Peachtree Street. She felt as
if her own roots had been dug up with those earth moving
machines—her foundation as toppled as the debris before her
eyes.

Since she was five years old, Alice worshipped there. From
the age of twelve she played piano for the youth program, while
for over twenty-five years her mother was pianist at worship
services. That church was a stronghold for Alice, an anchor in
a rapidly changing world. It was *home.*

And a beautiful home it was. Red bricks and white columns.
A true landmark, for seventy years it stood in regal dignity on a
lush lawn, its white steeple pointing all to God. Even so, some
of the congregation had decided it was time to move the church

to the suburbs and soon afterwards the vintage building was slated for destruction.

Alice recalled the members of the church—now scattered—who had become her extended family. In trying times, they were always there for her. In happy times they rejoiced with her. Their prayers followed her when she went away to college. *Those dear people are responsible in my being part of the Atlanta Symphony these thirty-five years!*

Instantly, her thoughts were back in Waco, Texas, when she was a graduate student at Baylor University. While agonizing over whether to major in piano or violin, Alice won an invitation to play violin with the *Dallas Symphony Orchestra*. She was elated. That is, she was until that day at rehearsal when the concertmaster said, "Alice, you play well. But if you plan to play professionally, you must have a better instrument than that cigar box you're playing."

Alice knew that money for an expensive instrument would be hard to come by. Her mother taught piano but her dad had suffered a stroke and was unable to continue with *his* work. Still her parents somehow managed her college tuition plus music lessons and to help out, Alice had a few music students of her own. Her mother encouraged her to shop around—to see if she could find a good violin at reasonable cost.

As it happened, Alice's teacher, Dr. James Barber, was from Philadelphia. "I know a top dealer there," he told her, "one of the oldest violin dealers in the world. Let me contact *William Moennig & Sons* and see if they will send you several instruments to try."

They sent four. But there was never a question. Right away Alice fell in love with the *Grancino*. Meticulously handcrafted in 1700 by Milan master Giovanni Grancino, it was the most beautiful thing she could imagine. A deep, rich caramel, its velvety patina spoke of loving hands—and loving hearts—which created it, and cared for it, through the centuries. What history it could tell if only it could talk! Yet *sing*, it *could*. Its hauntingly lovely voice filled a concert hall with the sweetest of song.

"Mother," Alice reported over the telephone, "it costs $4,000 (a huge sum in 1965). But if I had this violin, I could play the most beautiful music!"

"You must bring it home for us to see and hear."

Alice finished semester exams and flew home, the treasured violin in her lap for safekeeping. Exhausted, she wanted nothing more that night than to fall into bed. Her mother was having none of that. "No, Alice, we're going to mid-week prayer service. I want to hear you play the violin in the sanctuary."

Before the service began their pastor, Dr. Roy McClain, lovingly picked up the *Grancino*, ran his hand over its time-smoothed surface, and in an almost sacred tone, pronounced, "This instrument is a thing of rare beauty." A connoisseur of antiques, he knew that age and use are needed to mellow a violin to perfection. "Alice, I can hardly wait to hear you play it."

The moment Alice drew the bow across the strings and the sweet voice of the *Grancino* wafted over the sanctuary, faces in the audience took on a lovely glow. She knew it was a moment she would never forget. Nor would she ever forget what happened next.

Dr. McClain was about to close the service, when a lady stood and asked permission to speak. "I would like for us to say a special thank-you to Alice. I want her to know how very much we appreciate her talent and her volunteer work here through the years."

The pastor eagerly agreed. He paused a moment before continuing, "And may I add to that?" he said. "I can't help but see the concern on Alice's face at the possibility of giving up this violin." Another pause. "I'm wondering—if she really *has* to."

A hush fell over the congregation.

"I'm wondering," Dr. McClain went on, "if in order to express our appreciation for Alice as well as for her mother who has played the piano all these years without compensation, I'm wondering if we might just present the *Grancino* to Alice as our gift?"

Hands shot up, people made pledges, and in no time, the *Grancino* belonged to Alice. She could hardly believe it! She and her mother both almost cried. "There will be no coffee drinking around this violin," Alice said, promising to take good care of the precious gift.

She returned to college, feeling in her heart that the gift of the *Grancino* was God's way of telling her, "Alice, I want you to major in violin. I have a place of service for you." And sure enough, as soon as she completed her education, Alice and the *Grancino* auditioned for *The Atlanta Symphony Orchestra*, and began a wonderful thirty-five-years-and-counting adventure.

A few weeks after her tearful scene at the demolition site, at the Sunday morning service of a downtown church, Alice prepared the *Grancino* for her solo. Tenderly, she hugged the violin under her chin and positioned her left hand on the fingerboard. As she eased the bow across the strings, the full, luxurious tone of the *Grancino* soared upward.

Turning toward the congregation, her glance fell upon one of the women who had been part of the violin presentation in her home church many years earlier. In the woman's countenance, Alice sensed God speaking to her heart. "Alice, don't you see? My church is not a building. My church is my *people, wherever* they gather to worship me. Just remember, Alice, it's not where *you* are; it's where *I* am." The moment was so intense, she wondered if she might have even stopped playing.

Alice regained her composure, and was surprised to find her mind now at perfect peace. She caressed the dear old instrument and gave herself to the music—the particularly touching, meditative piece, *Borowski's Adoration.* Never had the *Grancino* sounded sweeter.

That experience changed her whole perspective. Now she knows that wherever the people have gone from her old congregation, their love undergirds her every day. And whether she's playing in a simple church or a European cathedral—an ornate concert hall or Atlanta's *Piedmont Park*—whenever she's among God's people worshipping Him, she's standing on holy ground. For she recalls God's message, "It's not where *you* are. It's where *I* am."

This, for Alice, was an *extra* gift and a special one indeed. She treasures it in her heart, even while she treasures the gift of the Grancino.

Semper Fi

*"Act with courage, and may the LORD be with
those who do well."*
2 Chronicles 19:11b, NIV

A young Marine helps his mother find courage—and renewed faith

The call came in the middle of a scorching Saturday afternoon. Our younger son Rick, stationed at Cherry Point Marine Corps Air Station in North Carolina, had been admitted to the hospital with a ruptured appendix. "They brought him down to Camp Lejeune and performed surgery," his friend reported, "but I can't find him."

Fear took over as I suspected the worse. *A ruptured appendix can prove fatal.* "We'll be there as soon as we can," I said, but we were two states away. *Oh, God, please help Rick.*

I called Joe in from mowing the lawn and, frantic, he phoned Camp Lejeune, locating the surgeon. "Yes, I operated on your son this morning," he said. "The infection had spread into the surrounding tissues. We're leaving the incision open in case we have to go back in there." *That means peritonitis has set in. Lord, help. My courage just vanished.*

"I have to tell you," the doctor added, "he is a very sick boy. But he's young; he's in good physical shape. I think he'll be able to make it." *Oh, Lord, give us all courage and strength.*

Joe never talks while driving, so I had practically all night to think—and worry.

Why in the world did Rick wait so long before seeing a doctor? Then my wandering mind reasoned: *Why am I surprised? The Marine Corps evidently teaches its men they can withstand anything—that they're invincible.*

I should know. Joe, himself, is a Marine to the core. *Semper Fidelis*—always faithful. He enlisted at age seventeen and now, with the rank of Major, served with a Reserve Unit in Atlanta. The fact that Rick followed in his dad's footsteps shouldn't have surprised me.

On the open road this night, the steady drone of car engine provided the only sound. Soon we were swallowed up in blackness, blackness relieved only by the streetlights of an occasional town, sleeping now.

Continuing my reverie, I contemplated the crucial factor that had influenced Rick, affected us *all* for that matter. Four years earlier, we had faced another surgical crisis when Joe was diagnosed with incurable cancer. Although he appeared to be beating the odds, the outcome as yet was uncertain. It had been particularly demoralizing for him when the Marine Corps declared him medically unfit to serve. Just recently, though, he had been reinstated to active status and even dared to hope for a promotion in rank.

This specter of uncertainty about his dad's health clouded the years Rick was in college. The week he received his degree, he had his hair cut short, shaved off his beard, and joined the Corps. "Somebody's got to carry on the tradition," he explained.

I recall vividly the heart-wrenching day he flew off for basic training at Officer Candidate School. After all, just twenty years earlier he was my little bundle of joy. Most mothers will tell you—we never fully give up feeling they're our babies. *Lord, help me once again to keep the faith in a crisis, to trust you in all things——even this.*

At three o'clock in the morning we reached the Camp Lejeune hospital, a soon-to-be-replaced red brick building of World War I vintage, three stories, dark now except for a smattering of dim lights on each floor.

Inside, our footsteps echoed down dismal hallways. A squeaky elevator emptied us onto the third floor where, at the far end, a small lamp revealed a desk and the silhouette of a nurse bent over her paper work. We approached her and asked about our son. She looked up, gave us the once-over, and said, ever so kindly, "Would you like to see him?"

"Oh, yes! May we?"

"Follow me," she said. With that, she picked up a flashlight, flicked it on, and cut us a path down the black asphalt-tiled floor of yet another gloomy corridor.

"He's in the room with another patient," the nurse said softly, motioning us through a door. "We'll need to be as quiet as possible."

We barely could detect Rick's bed in the shadows. Following the sounds of muted groans, being careful of the IV-dispensing contraption with its tubes and bottles, I touched his shoulder. His hospital gown was drenched with perspiration. "Rick," I whispered, bending close to his ear, "it's Mother and Dad."

A very groggy son answered, "I'm glad you're here."

I leaned over and kissed his fevered brow, "I love you."

"Love you, too," he managed. Then drifted back into a medicine-induced sleep.

Lord, our boy here needs your healing touch. And, Lord, about that courage—I need it now, real bad.

Rick was alert the next day—Sunday—but still feverish and miserable with pain.

On Monday morning, Joe let me out at the front door to the hospital while he found a parking space. The hallways, quiet all weekend, bustled now with activity. White-uniformed nurses and corpsmen hurried in and out of rooms; patients—all wearing U.S. Navy-issued blue cotton robes and scuffs—did their prescribed walking.

When I reached Rick's room, he lay flat on his back, anxiously eyeing the door. "Where's Dad?" he asked hurriedly, a note of excitement in his voice.

"He's parking the car."

"Can you help me get up?" he said, painfully pushing the sheet back with his feet and with great effort raising himself on one elbow, "I've got to be standing when Dad gets here."

I sensed this was no time for questions. Taking his arms while he clinched his teeth against the hurting, I pulled him around into a sitting position on the edge of the bed, then sat down beside him. While he held his incision with one hand, he placed the other one around my shoulder. I, in turn, put one arm around his back with my other hand steadying us with his IV pole, and somehow we stood to the floor. We propped the back of his legs against the bed for support. Then he motioned me to ease away.

Just in time. Masculine footsteps in the hall. "Sh-h-h."

Joe barely got inside the room when he stopped in his tracks, not believing what he saw: Rick, *standing* by his bed. Whereupon Rick pulled himself to almost-full height, snapped to attention, and with a crisp salute heralded, "Congratulations, Colonel, Sir!"

"Wha—wha—what?" Joe stammered, totally bewildered.

"Your promotion came through!" Rick reported, a big grin forming. "Col. Asher called this morning from Atlanta. *You're* a Lieutenant Colonel!!!"

"Promotion? Called here? How did he find me *here?*"

To describe Joe as dumbfounded would be a gross understatement. He was undone! Oh, but for a video camera to record the event. Suddenly, it all sank in and his face lit up like the fourth of July!

And just as suddenly, the Marine in him sprang back to life. With his officer demeanor engaged, he "snapped to," and—even though he was wearing civilian clothes which ruled out an official salute—returned Rick a quick, informal one. "Thank you, Lieutenant."

Then, with two long strides, Joe reached Rick and enfolded him in a giant bear hug. I joined in to make it a threesome. We laughed and cried, all at the same time, realizing that probably no promotion ever came at a more tender moment.

After we helped Rick back into bed, he furnished a perfect finish to the stirring scene. Reverting to his affectionate title for his dad, he said, "We're awfully proud of you, Pa."

Pa, the new Colonel. We were "just family" once again.

Yet, I dare say, a *changed* family. For etched forever in my heart is the picture of that young feverish Marine in a wrinkled, bob-tailed hospital gown, barely able to stand, snapping to attention and "promoting" his dad! What a memorable moment! What *courage*! Semper Fi—to the core!

I borrowed some of that courage the next day when Joe and I left for home, when our tear-mingled embraces followed three lump-throated goodbyes.

As we drove away, I felt at peace, confident that our boy would get well. The surgeon had pointed out that Rick was young and strong physically. Now, with that memorable moment, God had allowed me to see evidence of his *inner* strength as well. My faith was secure once again. God was looking after our son. And *me.*

Still, where was my faith, my courage, early on in this experience? And I am reminded of something I once read: "There are no yesterday leftovers of courage."

It is true—courage must be renewed daily.

And so must faith.

"Jesus"...in the Philippine Sand

[Jesus said] "... and you will be my witnesses in Jerusalem, and in all Judea and Samaria, and to the ends of the earth."
Acts 1:8b, NIV

Two college students give new meaning to the term "mission trip."

Down through the centuries God's people have heard His call, "Whom will I send? Who will go for us?"

And down through the centuries there have been those who answered, "Here am I. Send me" (Isaiah 6:8, NIV).

So it was that two college students from Georgia signed on with an interdenominational evangelistic group which was organizing in Mississippi. The group would devote their summer vacation to sharing the Gospel of Jesus Christ. Their mission field would be a remote area of the Philippine Islands. Excitedly, Greg Adams and Matt Turner prepared for their first real evangelistic work.

Their flight was scheduled to land at Pagadian, but the rainy son had left the airstrip under water. A typhoon raged nearby

268

as they made their way by boat across forty miles of choppy seas. One village on their itinerary had been heavily damaged by recent terrorists' burnings.

On Mindanao, Greg and Matt spent their days teaching and preaching in schools and churches. When they were introduced as being nineteen years old, the audience invariably reacted with surprise. "They thought we were much older," Greg explains.

Living with national families, Greg and Matt learned just how different living conditions can be. There was no electricity, no refrigeration.

Greg tells of one experience: "It was dark when we got to where I was staying, but I could tell the house was on stilts in the water. Still, I never expected what I saw when I woke the next morning. The tide was out, and under the house were walking fish!"

Matt describes the beds as being made of plywood with hard grass mats on top. "And they're made for Filipinos who are much shorter than we are."

The two young men were pleased to learn that approximately 80 percent of the people speak English. But the farther up in the mountains they visited, the more primitive they found the living conditions. And fewer people spoke English.

In one small village, or barrio, they stayed in a house under which the family kept chickens. "Every morning about 4:30 those chickens announced it was time to get up," Matt tells with a grin. "One morning at first rooster call, two ladies in the house got up and—in their native language—sang a duet. Then all was quiet again."

Then there was the basketball game to end all basketball games. It seems that original plans had called for a college basketball team to travel with the group. They were to play exhibition games. While the crowd was gathered, the missionary group would share the gospel with them. But alas, the team was not along on the trip.

Nevertheless, at one stop a professional Filipino basketball team had assembled to play the visiting team from America. Not wishing to disappoint them, Greg and Matt along with two high school teachers and an 18-year-old from Mississippi took them on.

Up until now, all the nationals whom the group had seen were relatively short. Imagine their astonishment to see the team come out on the court—all six footers! And with many substitute players!

Greg says, "Toward the end of the second half, we were all but exhausted. On impulse I said to the opponent nearest me, 'Do you know something? My mother's an excellent cook! If you're ever in the United States, stop by and you can eat some of the best food you've ever tasted!"

Other members of the temporary team joined in the chatter. Soon the professional team showed their good sportsmanship by playing along with this "new game." The "missionary five" were allowed to catch up to within eight points of the score before the pros got serious again.

"At halftime, we had our opportunity to address the spectators," Matt says. "I explained to them that in the United States, Greg and I weren't basketball players—we played football. Yet we were willing to do anything to get to tell people about Jesus."

When the day came to say good-bye to their new friends on Mindanao, Greg and Matt walked down to the beach. Carefully they printed on the black sand: *JESUS.* The tide was coming in, slowly rolling a sheet of water over the letters. Soon the picture would be gone—yet, they hoped, not forgotten. Greg and Matt pray the name of Jesus will live forever in the hearts of the people—the people of the Philippines.

Teacher At Last

As written for: Eugene Edwards

"Hold fast to dreams, for if dreams die,
life is a broken winged bird that cannot fly."
Langston Hughes (1902-1967)
American Poet, Author, Playwright

"If you dream long enough—and work hard enough
—the good Lord will help make your dream come true."
Eugene Edwards, *Teacher At Last.*

I pulled on my black overcoat, stepped outside into a cold, January afternoon, and paused. *Well, Atlas Plumbing Company, I've spent thirty years of my life turning you into a successful business. Now I must follow my heart.* I shut the door for the last time and hung the sign: GONE OUT OF BUSINESS.

Climbing into my '91 Burgundy Explorer, at age fifty I turned all thoughts toward my life-long dream of being a schoolteacher. *Lord, you've brought me this far,* I pleaded, *please don't leave me now.*

While driving home, I wished Mr. Roy was still alive so we could discuss it. Mr. Roy was my mentor, my role model. Mr. Roy *talked* with me, asked me questions. Just like I was *somebody* instead of a scrawny little black kid.

I was about six when we found each other in Mayfield, South Carolina, where I was born. There was a little family-run store in our neighborhood. Out front the American flag waved right next to the Coca-Cola sign above the screen door. Mr. Roy and some other old-timers usually were there, propped on upside-down nail kegs next to the pot-bellied stove, playing a round of checkers and swapping yarns.

Every day after school I sidled up by the checkerboard—to "help out" Mr. Roy with his game. And it was there, at Mr. Roy's elbow, that many of my values were born.

Not that my parents didn't teach me things. They did. But as there were 17 of us children at home, *individual* attention was hard to come by.

"Eugene," Mr. Roy said one day, "whatta' you wanna' be when you grow up?"

"A teacher," I fairly blurted out.

In a tone which left no room for doubt Mr. Roy responded, "Then be one!"

Mr. Roy could see the pitfalls ahead. "Eugene," he said, dead serious as he wrapped one bony arm around my equally thin shoulders, "There will be times when folks will say, `You can't do that.' Just take that in stride. Then set out to prove 'em wrong."

During my junior year of high school, Mom passed away and Dad needed me to help care for the younger children. As college was now out of the question, I put aside my teacher dream and took up a trade instead—plumbing.

I recalled another of Mr. Roy's admonitions. "One more thing, Eugene," he'd said. "Whatever you become, whether you're a ditch-digger or a school teacher, you be the best you can be. That's all the good Lord asks of us."

So I told myself, *If I can't be a teacher, I'll be the best plumber in the business.* I learned all I could about the trade. Practiced what I believed—*Do it right the first time and you don't have to go back.* Eventually I had my own business.

Meanwhile, Annette and I married and reared two fine children. Now Michael was completing his PhD, Monique was a college senior, while Annette had gone back to school several years earlier and made a fine teacher.

Now that day had come when my dream no longer would be denied. Four days after I closed my shop, I started work at Hendrix Drive Elementary School. Not as a teacher, mind you, but as custodian. I traded my wrenches and pipe fittings for brooms and paintbrushes. And a 40% reduction in pay. I figured the job would be a good way to test the waters—to see if I could even relate to the youngsters of today.

I hit it off with the students. In the hallways while running the floor polisher, I'd throw them a big high five and each responded with wide grin and a "five back-at-you."

Often I found a youngster propped up against the wall outside his classroom, having been banished there for misbehavior. "What'za matter, son?" I'd ask him, truly concerned. After he had related his current infraction of rules and I had emphasized his need to comply, I'd go in and talk with his teacher, smoothing the way for a return to the classroom.

Surprisingly, I made a very fine mediator. Maybe because I could put myself in the mindset of these youngsters. So many—like my young friend Jeffrey—come from broken homes, being raised by their single mom, or by a grandmother. They are *hungry* for a positive male role model, someone who will show genuine interest in them, show them they are loved. They desperately need a Mr. Roy in *their* lives. I wanted to be that one.

Sometimes, too, that means being strict. More than once I pulled a young man over to the side of the hallway and reprimanded him about his baggy pants with no belt, the waist dragging down around his knees, underwear showing. In fact, that's how I had met Jeffrey.

"Wait right here," I told him. From my supply closet I brought a length of venetian blind cord to run through his belt loops. The next day, Jeffrey came to school wearing a belt. So did the other boys when it came *their* turn for correction. Unorthodox behavior for a custodian? Maybe. But the kids respected my opinion because they knew I *cared.*

I did a lot of thinking, and praying, while I polished those floors. *I have a ministry right here as a custodian,* I rationalized. *Maybe I don't need to put myself through the rigors of college courses in order to help students.*

All the while, I could hear Mr. Roy saying, "Never settle for second best, Eugene. Whatever you become, you be the best you can be."

One night I ventured to the family, "Looks like I'm gonna' have to go to college after all."

They said, "Go for it!"

So I did. In the fall I registered for night and weekend courses at the Norcross branch of Brenau University. I plain had the jitters when I approached those first classes. *Will I be the oldest student there? Am I too old, too tired to learn those tough subjects?*

On top of those worries, working all day then studying until 2 a.m. only to get up at 5:30 was rough. While cleaning those floors, I carried on a running dialogue with God. "Lord, I'm bone weary. Remind me again that this is something *You* want me to do. 'Cause I tell you the truth, if it's just *my* wanting it, I'm about ready to quit."

In answer, I believe God sent Jeffrey back to me. Jeffrey had graduated from our school the year before; now he came to visit and found me about to replace a fluorescent bulb in a hallway. "Jeffrey, I am so glad to see you!" I said, while giving him a big bear hug. "How're you doing, son?"

"Fine, Sir," he responded, his good manners impressing me beyond measure. "Mr. Edwards," he went on, "I want to thank you for the time you spent with me here, for caring about me. I never would have made it through sixth grade if it had not been for you."

"Jeffrey, I am so proud of you," I responded. "And you're going to finish high school, aren't you?"

"Yes, Sir," he said, his face breaking into a huge smile, "I'm even going to college, Mr. Edwards! Like *you!*"

I almost cried. I determined to stick it out with my studies. Jeffrey was counting on me.

Now it is early morning—May 3, 1997—a day that will go down in history. Today is *graduation day!*

At Gainesville's *Georgia Mountain Center*, I almost am overcome with emotion. Standing outside in my black robe, mortarboard with tassel atop my head, I glance at the blue-stoned college class ring on this fifty-five-year-old plumber's work-worn hand. Tears threaten to run off down my cheeks.

As the music swells, the processional begins with Brenau University's president and faculty in full academic regalia looking impressive indeed, along with trustees and guest speaker: The Honorable Edward E. Elson, United States Ambassador to the kingdom of Denmark.

All those dignitaries remain standing to honor *us* as we file in—350 Evening and Weekend College Undergraduates, candidates for degrees. When I hear my name echoing throughout the huge hall—*EUGENE EDWARDS*—somehow I get up onto the stage, never feeling my feet touch the floor!

I float back to my seat, beaming like a lit-up Christmas tree, clutching the tangible evidence of a long-dreamed dream come true: a square of parchment with those all-important words, **Bachelor of Science Degree in Middle Grades Education.**

Yessiree, my inner self is thinking, *'just goes to show you. If you dream long enough—and work hard enough—the good Lord will help make your dream come true.*

A teacher at last!

Mr. Roy would be proud.

This Butterfly Soars Free

"So if the Son sets you free, you will be free indeed."
John 8:36, NIV

Sequel to "Who, Me? Walk on Water!" The author tells of her changed life.

As a new author, I had just made one of my first guest appearances on a nation-wide telecast. As the house lights came back on, a lady from the studio audience approached me. "You didn't look at all scared," she said.

"Thank you," I said, marveling at the truth of it. Plainly, a transformation had taken place, for I had been plagued with timidity all my life.

I still hurt with the humiliation of a first-grade incident. I was tongue-tied and painfully shy. When the teacher asked me to go down the hall and request the piano be brought to our room, the janitor never understood what I told him. Instead he thought I wanted a turn ringing the bell to start the school day. He lifted me up so I could reach the button high on the wall. My embarrassment knew no bounds when I returned to the classroom without the piano.

It didn't help that my home life was far from stable. My alcoholic father went on wild rampages when he was drinking and I often feared for my life. Growing up in that environment failed to foster the building of self-confidence.

When I was nine, Mother managed to move us across state, leaving Daddy behind. For the first time, I could attend Sunday School. I quickly learned to love this Jesus person they talked about. But I couldn't believe He loved *me*. Never having experienced a father's love, I felt unworthy of love.

Yet, I desperately sought love, approval. After Joe and I married and our two sons were born, finally I felt complete. With my family around me, in the safety of our home, I enjoyed the security I had lacked as a child.

That security was threatened one bitter-cold February day. As the hospital attendants maneuvered Joe's gurney into the hallway, he reached out to me. Our hands clasped briefly. There was little we could say—we didn't know what he was facing in surgery. "Please, God, be with him. Be with the doctors. Be with us who wait."

With each hour of waiting, my anxiety increased. "Please, God ..."

At last, Dr. Brown appeared, his green surgical mask hanging loosely around his neck. "We removed a malignant mass," he said.

Cancer! My worst fear had become a reality!

Groping for reassurance, I asked, "Did you get it all?"

He answered a gentle," No, we just couldn't."

That's when it happened. I felt myself begin to reel, too weak to reach out, even to God. But God, in his divine love, reached out to me. Suddenly I was aware of his presence in that room. Two mighty, yet very gentle arms seemed to appear from a haze at ceiling height. Swathed in loose-fitting white sleeves, the hands reached down for me as if to say, "Come, let me help you."

I fell into those arms and there I stayed. Whereupon I was lifted up and above all that was going on as God wrapped me in a cocoon of His love. For months I remained in almost a state of suspended animation, like the chrysalis hanging from a limb.

Joe underwent sickening chemotherapy, then debilitating radiation treatments. I fulfilled my role as wife and caregiver, doing my fair share of worrying. Yet, I felt like an onlooker to a scenario that involved someone who looked exactly like me.

Some might suggest I was in a state of shock. Of denial. Whatever the case, it was a time of spiritual growth. I was so touched by the Lord's coming to me in my hour of need, I sought to know Him better. I searched the Bible, listened to sacred songs on the radio, even read through the hymnbook.

At the same time, convinced that miracles still happen, I sought help for Joe's life from the Great Physician. I prayed, almost constantly I prayed.

I didn't realize a metamorphosis was taking place in *me*. For just as from the outside of a chrysalis it appears that nothing is happening, within its protective prison a delicate process is transforming a caterpillar into a butterfly.

Finally, we reached the one-year-since-cancer mark. Joe's prognosis still was poor but, at least, for the time being, his treatments were behind us. All at once, my cocoon burst open and a new me emerged into the light, still weak from struggle but with God-given wings beginning to unfurl!

About that time, Joe—concerned for my future—suggested I go back to school. After much prayer for guidance and with much trepidation, I returned to college, a first quarter sophomore after an absence of twenty-seven years!

In the middle of my junior year, I sensed again the Lord was speaking to me. One morning while dressing for class, I saw in my mind's eye the word JOURNALISM, in big, bold black letters. I doggedly pursued my social work studies.

For six months I dared argue with God. But I became miserable! Finally I could take it no more. I went into my bedroom, fell to my knees, and cried out to Him. "Lord, I don't understand it, but I'll do it." I changed my major field of study to journalism.

The day I received that degree from Brenau University, I didn't walk down the aisle, I *floated*, wings waving in the wind. And miracle of miracles, Joe was there to cheer me on.

Then I went home to become the writer God wanted me to be. After five more years of individual study, work, and rejection slips, *Tyndale House* published my book *THE HEALING, One Family's Victorious Struggle With Cancer*.

Overnight it changed me from a rather quiet, stay-at-home wife and mother to a small-town celebrity-of-sorts. I spent a year traveling—from Georgia to California to Toronto—appearing on television, being interviewed on radio programs, making speeches and enjoying book signings.

I can still see the looks on the faces of Randy and Rick when they first saw Mom autographing her book. Their expressions said *I can't believe this is our mother!* Neither could I.

That's how I felt, too, when I won *Guideposts'* weeklong workshop. Sitting in their New York offices, I had to pinch myself to see if I was dreaming. Years later, even after many published pieces, I still get excited each time an article of mine appears in print.

Yet, as thrilling as my writing career has been, the changes within have been even more so. The overriding one is my feeling of self-worth. When I learned that God loves me, *I* could love me too. That freed me to love others. And that love flows back to me, over and over.

I recall another of my television appearances. After the program a fellow guest said, "You blessed me before we even went on the air."

Me? A blessing! Oh I do hope so. It would be my small way of saying "Thank you, Lord." For God took my painful past and gave me a glorious life. Truly, He is the wind beneath my wings.

I like to think He takes pleasure in seeing the results as

this

butterfly

soars

free.

EDITOR' NOTE: Gloria Cassity Stargel recounts "the rest of the story" in her award-winning book *THE HEALING, One Family's Victorious Struggle with Cancer.* Other portions of the Stargel family's story are found in this volume: "Who, Me? Walk on Water!" "This Marine's Wakeup Call," "Mine Eyes Have Seen the Glory," "O Blessed Warmth," "After Winter, Spring." The Healing is available at www.brightmorning.com.

Epilogue: God's Love

We can only see a little of the ocean,
A few miles distant from the rocky shore;
But out there—beyond, beyond our eyes' horizon,
There's more—there's more.

We can only see a little of God's loving—
A few rich treasures from His mighty store:
But out there—beyond, beyond our eyes' horizon,
There's more—there's more!

Anonymous

The Best Loved Religious Poems
James Gilchrist Lawson, Fleming H. Revell Company © 1933

Help for Your Journey

I hope you've enjoyed our stories. More than that, I hope you've found inspiration and encouragement for your own journey as you sail the sea of life. For there is nothing to compare with the security gained when you place your trust in Jesus—and your anchor holds.

HOW TO BECOME A CHRISTIAN

Do *you* know Jesus? If not, I invite you to meet Him now. Accepting Jesus as Lord is a win-win situation: eternal life with Him, plus abundant life here. The Bible tells us: "For God so loved the world that He gave His one and only Son, that whoever believes in Him shall not perish but have eternal life" (John 3:16, NIV). And Jesus said, "I have come that they may have life, and have it to the full" (John 10:10b, NIV).

Even with such awesome results, the process is quite simple: It's a matter of faith, of trust—trust in Jesus who willingly gave His life for all those who will believe.

So, just talk to God, an awesome privilege in itself. Tell Him you want to accept Jesus as Lord of your life. Ask Him to forgive you of all wrongdoing. He will answer your prayer and send His Holy Spirit to live within you. And your life will never be the same.

I pray that you will know Jesus—and the difference He makes.

Gloria

About the Author

G loria Cassity Stargel is an author, free-lance writer and an
assignment writer for Guideposts magazine. A born-again
Christian, she is dedicated to sharing with others the good news
of Jesus Christ.

Her book *The Healing, "One Family's Victorious Struggle
with Cancer,"* Tyndale House Publishers and Bright Morning
Publications, earned the "Award for Excellence in Writing" at
the Blue Ridge Christian Writers Conference, Black Mountain,
North Carolina.

Mrs. Stargel's award-winning articles have been published
in dozens of periodicals, among them: Home Life, Journal
of Christian Nursing; and Decision, published by the Billy
Graham Evangelistic Association. Other articles are in an equal
number of anthologies, including *Chicken Soup for the Soul,
God Answers Prayers, Stories for the Heart, Grace Givers ...*

A member of National League American Pen Women,
North Georgia Writers, Beta Sigma Phi International Sorority,
Mu Rho Sigma, and Phi Beta Sigma Honor Society, Mrs. Stargel
holds a degree in Social Work/Journalism. She is a 2003 inductee
into the Brenau University Alumni Hall of Fame.

You are invited to visit her website at www.brightmorning.
com.

Permissions to Reprint

Except those so noted, all copyrights are in the name of Gloria Cassity Stargel.

CHAPTER I: CAPTAIN

"Ugly Car, Pretty Girl, and Mr. Pridgen" first appeared in *Decision, 2001*, Billy Graham Evangelistic Association, reprinted by permission of the author.

"By Way of Hope" excerpted from Feature Article "Mr. B," *The Times*, Gainesville, GA, Sept. 7, 2003, © *The Times*, used by permission.

"The Day Cheering Stopped" first appeared in *Stories for a Teen's Heart, Multnomah Publishers*, 2002, reprinted by permission of the author.

"Rickey's Perfect Gift" first appeared in *Singing News Magazine*, Sept. 1998, reprinted by permission of the author.

"This Marine's Wakeup Call," under title "No Time to Live," first appeared in *God's Way for Fathers*, White Stone Books, 2003, reprinted by permission of the author.

"To Alaska, With Love" first appeared in *The Times*, Gainesville, GA, Jan. 26, 1997. © *The Times*, used by permission.

CHAPTER 2: LIGHTHOUSE

"Harmony Restored," under title "I Almost Missed the Sunset," first appeared in *The Ministers' Family,* Summer 2000. Used by permission of the author.

"Lesson in Grace" first appeared in *God's Way for Teachers,* 2004, reprinted by permission of the author.

"Sweet Sixteen" first appeared in *WITH,* March 1996, reprinted by permission of the author.

CHAPTER 3: ANCHOR

"That Night in May," 2003, © *Guideposts for Teens,* Book Rights reserved. Used by permission of the author.

"Girl Who Lost Her Smile" Apr. 2000. © *Guideposts for Teens,* Book Rights reserved. Used by permission of the author.

"Death of a Village" first appeared as one part of a three-part series in *The Times,* Gainesville, GA, Aug. 1990, © *The Times,* used by permission.

"For Such a Time as This" first appeared in *Their Mysterious Ways,* Guideposts Books, 2002, reprinted by permission of the author.

CHAPTER 4: HOPE

"To Tie My Son's Shoes" first appeared in *Contact,* Mar. 1981, reprinted by permission of the author.

Portions of "After Winter—Spring," first appeared in *The Healing, One Family's Victories Struggle With Cancer,* Tyndale House Publishers, 1982, reprinted by permission of the author.

"When Prayers Take Twists and Twines," first appeared in *Mature Years,* Winter 2005-06, reprinted by permission of the author.

"Flight for Freedom" first appeared in *God Answers Prayers Military Edition*, Harvest House, 2005, reprinted by permission of the author.

"The Day My Son Became a Marine," under title "Faith Is Trust" first appeared in *Standard, Nazarene*, Nov. 25, 1984, reprinted by permission of the author.

"Package Deal" first appeared in *God's Way for Women*, White Stone Books, 2003, reprinted by permission of the author.

"Crisis on the Court" first appeared in *Chicken Soup for the Christian Woman's Soul*, 2004, reprinted by permission of the author

CHAPTER 5: LIFELINE

"Mine Eyes Have Seen The Glory" first appeared as Chapter 19 of *The Healing*, reprinted by permission of the author.

"Rescue of Little Naomi," first appeared as "Angels Watching Over Little Nancy," *God Answers Prayers*, Harvest House Publishers, 2005, reprinted by permission of the author.

"The Night An Angel Sang" first appeared as "Alone" in *Chicken Soup for the Christian Soul 2*, 2005, reprinted by permission of the author.

"Home for Christmas" first appeared in *God's Way for Fathers*, 2003, reprinted by permission of the author.

"Devastation at Dawn" First Appeared in *Christian Reader*, Mar/Apr 2002, reprinted by permission of the author.

CHAPTER 6: REFUGE

"The Peacekeeper" first appeared in *Ripples of Joy*, A Shaw Book, 2000, reprinted by permission of the author.

CHAPTER 7: POWER